# Learning-focused Supervision:

Developing Professional Expertise
in Standards-Driven Systems

by Laura Lipton, Ed.D and Bruce Wellman, M.Ed

The Road To Learning
www.miravia.com

MiraVia, Charlotte, VT

# Learning-focused Supervision:

## Developing Professional Expertise in Standards-Driven Systems

by Laura Lipton, Ed.D and Bruce Wellman, M.Ed

Permission for some materials in this book has been granted by the authors and/or publishers.

Every effort has been made to appropriately cite original sources. We apologize for any oversights in obtaining permission and would be happy to rectify them in future printings.

10 9 8 7 6 5 4

Fourth printing, November 2013

Printed in the United States of America
ISBN 978-0-9665022-8-2  Softcover

MiraVia, LLC
236 Lucy's Lane  Charlotte VT 05445
www.miravia.com

# Contents

# 1. Assumptions about Learning-focused Supervision

Teacher learning links directly to student learning. Several lines of research confirm that skillful forms of supervision influence teacher commitment and personal efficacy (Ebmeier, 2003, Tschannen-Moran, Hoy & Hoy,1998). Given the pace of change in schools with shifts in student demographics, curriculum updates, and new instructional approaches, teaching must be the learning profession. To support the professional growth of teachers, supervisors need templates and tools for guiding their interactions with staff members.

*How* supervisors interact with teachers is as important as the *what* of those interactions. The thoughtful use of many types of data is the foundation for learning-focused interactions. Clearly understood and agreed upon evaluative criteria are the reference points that enable supervisors to provide specific feedback to teachers. Such standards and rating scales describing levels of effectiveness support gap analysis, goal setting and ultimately, independent self-assessment on the part of teachers regarding their performance.

The more actively engaged teachers are in the evaluation process, the more learning will occur and the greater the commitment to that learning. This process requires conversations between supervisors and teachers that are focused on growth, not remediation or repair. In this way, the conversation moves from *"How did I do?"* to *"How can I get better?"* (Sartain, et al. 2011).

For supervisors, the ability to structure and facilitate powerful learning-focused conversations lies at the heart of both one-on-one and collective work with teachers. Standards, (see for example, Danielson, 2011; Marzano, 2011; Marshall, 2011) provide the *what* to talk about; learning-focused supervision offers the *how* for structuring these conversations.

## Four Qualities of Learning-focused Supervision

Learning-focused supervision is a growth-oriented process that encompasses four key qualities. This approach to building capacity is developmental, standards-driven, data-based and customized.

## Developmental

Learning-focused supervision is a developmental process. Growth-oriented supervisors are goal driven, working with teachers to build their capacity to self-monitor, self-manage and self-modify their practice for continuous improvement. They see teachers as they might be and project these positive images for success into their interactions with staff members. Such supervisors view current performance levels as starting points not ceilings.

**Learning-focused Supervision is:**

- Developmental
- Standards-driven
- Data-based
- Customized

## Standards-driven

Standards frame shared expectations and establish and clarify measures of excellence for teacher and student performance. Used effectively, they become rallying points for important conversations about instructional practice and the results of teaching choices. By focusing on these ideals, learning-focused interactions become conversations about desired results and any gaps between present performance and those results — not about personal failings on the part of the teacher.

## Data-based

Objective data ground conversations in concrete images of teacher and student behaviors and performance. The quality of these data matter greatly. Literal notes, student work products and other forms of information focus the conversation on tangible evidence that becomes a catalyst for exploration and analysis. These data then become the foundation for calibrating performance against clear standards, stimulating goal setting and the clarification of desirable and measurable results.

## Customized

Learning-focused supervision is a customized process. During planning and reflecting conversations, skilled supervisors apply teaching and learning standards to the context of the practitioner. They illuminate and clarify expectations using examples based on the teaching assignment, grade level or content area. They incorporate and consider time of year, years of teaching experience and any current initiatives being implemented. By attending to the individual needs of teachers, skillful supervisors personalize their adult learning relationships to create safe environments for risk-taking. Flexibility with language, learning style and teaching models as well as facility with the full array of supervisory templates and tools described in this book provide the essential resources for helping teachers stretch, grow, and see themselves as capable learners of the art and science of teaching.

## Assumptions Informing Learning-focused Supervision

In a learning-focused supervisory process, high quality, data-driven feedback stimulates teachers' thinking about their work. To support the professional growth of teachers, learning-focused supervisors apply standards and structures for guiding their interactions with staff members. These patterns and practices initiate and sustain teacher learning that is guided by student learning needs. This approach is based on the following four assumptions.

### 1. Teaching is complex and contextual.

Teaching is a complex craft. Skillful teachers manage the social, emotional and academic needs of increasingly diverse student populations. Total classroom awareness requires attention to these three dimensions while simultaneously tracking the lesson plan, content accuracy, use of examples, clarity of explanations and directions and choice of language to match student readiness. These teachers provide relevant and meaningful tasks, attend to momentum and pacing while purposefully monitoring student understanding, making adjustments as needed. And all of this is orchestrated for individual students, small groups and the full class.

All of this work is done in an ever-shifting context inside and outside the classroom. These dynamics include changing politics and policies, shifting societal expectations, breakthroughs in the science of teaching and learning, ever-expanding content knowledge, and new technological tools that increase access to information.

**Consider:**

- What are some contextual factors that are influencing your work?

- What are some ways that supervisory practice in your work setting reflects the complexity of teaching?

### 2. Research-based standards define effective teaching.

Well-articulated standards reflect the complexity of professional practice. These detailed descriptions provide common language and reference points for talking about teaching in a variety of domains. Clear standards organized by levels of performance foster shared agreement between teachers and supervisors about the qualities of effective teaching. A robust body of research clearly demonstrates that highly rated teachers produce high performing students.

Thoughtful and thorough depictions of teacher actions and student behaviors establish the foundation for meaningful conversations about and improvements of instructional practice. High quality, standards-driven feedback establishes growth targets for teachers across the range of teaching skills.

**Consider:**

- What are some ways that conversations informed by clear and shared standards influence (or might influence) improvements in teaching practice and student learning?

### 3. Supervision is a growth-oriented process.

Learning-focused supervision is a developmental approach to supporting teacher learning. Like effective teachers, skillful supervisors differentiate their practice to increase expertise and support growth across novice to more expert career stages. This growth-orientation guides in-the-moment choices as supervisors draw from a rich repertoire of strategies to meet teachers' immediate needs.

Skillful teaching takes years to master. There are always areas for growth. The primary goal of supervision is to increase teachers' capacity to reflect on their own practice, self-assess, set goals and monitor for continuous improvement.

**Consider:**

- How does this developmental approach to supervision compare with present practices in your work setting?

### 4. The deepest purpose of supervision is to create a culture of learning.

A learning culture in schools makes knowledge public, spreads good ideas and energizes best practices. This reflective and inquiry-driven environment increases shared understanding of effective practice and provides a wide range of perspectives for examining critical issues. Learning-focused supervisory interactions create essential feedback loops that reinforce these values and amplify high expectations for all: students, teachers and supervisors.

Effective instructional leadership matters. Supervisors need to see themselves as learners and to believe in their own capacity and the capacity of others to grow. For supervisors, the ability to structure and facilitate learning-focused conversations lies at the heart of both one-on-one and collective work with teachers.

**Consider:**

- What are some things in your work setting that promote a culture of learning?

- What are some things that get in the way?

# 2. Four Stances: The Continuum of Learning-focused Interaction

In learning-focused conversations, accomplished supervisors shift between four stances: calibrating, consulting, collaborating, and coaching to develop teachers' capacities to reflect upon data, to generate ideas and options, and to increase personal and professional awareness and skill. Versatility across this continuum of interaction supports supervisory practices that are developmentally and contextually appropriate for serving the learning needs of teachers across a range of skill and experience. The ultimate aim of each of these stances and their cumulative effect is to support continuous learning on the part of teachers and to enhance their capacity to engage in productive collegial relationships.

Three attributes ultimately define the supervisory stance in any learning-focused conversation. One defining trait is the way that information emerges during the interaction. The second defining trait is the source of problem definition and gap analysis related to differences between planned goals and actual results, or learning standards and student performance. The third defining trait is the source of goals for teacher growth.

## The Continuum of Learning-focused Interaction

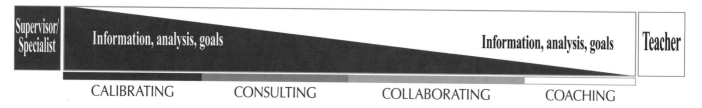

## Three Supervisory Capacities: Fluency, Flexibility and Fluidity

The skillful learning-focused supervisor draws upon three important capacities when navigating the continuum; fluency, flexibility, fluidity.

*Fluency of interaction.* Fluent supervisors recognize that they have choices in their approach to supervisory conversations. They are clear about the definition and purpose of each of the four stances and are able to operate across them, with a repertoire of strategies for each.

*Flexibility of interaction.* Flexible supervisors understand that different individuals and different contexts require different approaches. These supervisors have internalized criteria for choosing a given stance in a given situation and are able to be responsive to the teacher's immediate cognitive and emotional needs while being mindful of the ultimate goal of development over time.

*Fluidity of interaction.* Fluid supervisors are able to skillfully apply the continuum, seamlessly shifting stances as needed. They attend to both verbal and nonverbal cues from colleagues; listening and responding strategically. These supervisors have a level of automaticity that supports their ability to attend and respond to complexities and nuances, drawing upon a wide repertoire of knowledge and skill to make the match that produces the most learning in the moment.

There is a sequence to the development of these capacities as they build upon one another. Fluent supervisors become flexible as they expand their skill sets to include differentiated practice and the ability to monitor goals for teachers' development over time. As their integrated skill set becomes more sophisticated and nuanced, flexible supervisors can pay attention and construct responses with increased fluidity.

## The Four Stances

In professional conversations, supervisors apply standards and communicate expectations as they support teachers in using data to determine performance gaps and establish goals for improving practice. Learning-focused supervisors operate across a continuum of interaction to accomplish these responsibilities.

In each stance, the approach to these functions differs, as does the internal question supervisors consider when determining which stance to apply.

### Calibrating

In the calibrating stance, the guiding question is, *"What are the gaps/growth areas indicated for this teacher based on present performance levels and the standards?"*

In a learning-focused supervisory relationship, the calibrating stance is the stance of judgment. Based on a variety of data sources, the supervisor determines a level of performance and organizes the data and the conversation to inform and discuss this assessment with the teacher. It is the part of the conversation when the supervisor presents and explains his or her thinking about the teacher's level of performance. This stance is necessary when a teacher is unable to analyze his or her own practice and any gaps between current performance and desired standards. For example, a supervisor might provide data and highlight examples of distinguished practice to motivate and clarify goals for a developing or proficient teacher who lacks a vision for professional growth.

In the most extreme cases, the calibrating stance becomes the dominant stance in the conversation, with the greater percentage of time spent there. Some triggers for this choice include: teaching behaviors that create an unsafe or harmful environment physically or emotionally, teacher responses that are inappropriate, classroom management that is non-existent, student performance that is consistently below expectations and instructional planning and delivery that is ineffective. Calibrating is also an effective stance for motivating effective teachers to set goals for achieving higher levels of performance.

#### Functions

In the calibrating stance, the supervisor defines and reinforces teaching standards and expectations. The verb to calibrate means an active process of matching an object or performance to an agreed upon value. Simplistically, that value might be a shoe size or

Four Stances: The Continuum of Learning-focused Interaction

the diameter of a section of tubing. In contemporary educational discourse such values are expressed as standards. Important standards include creating a learning environment of respect and rapport, managing classroom procedures and student behaviors, communicating effectively with students, parents and colleagues, engaging students in meaningful learning and demonstrating flexibility and responsiveness based on assessment of student performance.

To operate with integrity within a calibrating stance the conversation must be driven by data. These data are used to identify gaps between expected standards and the present results, and/or to reinforce and illuminate effective practices and establish professional learning goals. Clearly articulating the standards and accessing available resource materials, learning-focused supervisors define and illuminate problems. They present models and examples of such standards in action that are content and grade level specific and explicitly name expectations. In planning for action, skillful supervisors determine achievable goals, success criteria and timelines for completion.

*Follow up is important*

---

### Calibrating

Principal Robinson has conducted two informal walk-throughs and a classroom observation of Mr. Miller's fourth grade class. In each case, two-thirds of Mr. Miller's students are out of their seats for much of the instructional period. Mr. Miller sits behind his desk and shouts at them to settle down. After 15 minutes, when they do take their seats, only a handful of students follow directions and participate in the lesson. Mr. Miller's questions require only factual recall, and are rapid-fire with no wait time.

Based on these classroom visits, Principal Robinson organizes her observation data and prepares for applying a calibrating stance. When she joins Mr. Miller, she begins:

"Given my observations of your classroom, there are two key areas that need to be addressed at this time: the first is managing classroom procedures and the second is questioning and discussion techniques. I've observed your classroom on three separate occasions and as these data indicate there are clear patterns that students are inattentive, there seem to be no clear procedures or effective interventions."

(She refers to the time-coded script of the teacher's language and the students' actions).

"At this point in the year, students should be clear about behavioral expectations. Specific procedures need to be in place, and your students should understand consequences for violating them. Transitions from one subject to the next should be smooth and take no longer than two minutes, with students in their seats with materials ready."

[Principal Robinson shifts to consultation and elaborates a menu of strategies for addressing these concerns, then directs Mr. Miller to choose one, or several for his action plan].

"The second area for improvement relates to questioning and discussion techniques. The scripted data indicate only recall questions with one second or less for students to respond. You answered eight of the fourteen questions yourself. Further, there were no strategies for distributed student response, such as signals, partners or choral response."

(Again, she makes the data available to Mr. Miller)

"Effective questions require learners to think and reflect, to deepen their understanding, to support their answers with evidence and to test their ideas against those of their classmates. To construct thoughtful responses to these questions, students need at least three-five seconds of wait time. She refers to the data, drawing his attention to the observation notes. "Right here, for example, was an opportunity to ask Rachel for elaboration. And here, students might have signaled agree or disagree."

The conversation continues as Principal Robinson names specific goals, identifies necessary next steps and establishes a timeline for achievement.

In most cases, the calibrating stance then leads to a rich conversation, shifting among the other stances. When used with chronically low-performing teachers or teachers who appear not to be "getting it," this stance is the most prescriptive of the four. Follow-up and follow through on the part of the supervisor are vital to ensure standards are being interpreted appropriately, performance targets are clear and student progress is occurring. Taking this stance may be necessary when other approaches are not producing the evidence of the transfer of the teacher's learning into improved classroom practices that produce positive changes in student actions and outcomes.

### Cautions

For each stance there are potential pitfalls. In the calibrating stance, it is easy for our personal preferences to become prescriptions. It is critical then, that any judgments are data based and standards driven, supported by clear, external criteria and evidence.

Avoid subjectivity or bias by using literal observation notes, specific classroom artifacts and assessment data. Supervisors' inferences or interpretations can increase the teachers' potential perceptions of personal attack.

## Consulting

In the consulting stance, the guiding question is, *"What information, ideas and technical resources will be most useful to this teacher at this time?"*

Based on the teacher's responses to initial inquiries, the supervisor recognizes gaps in content knowledge, student knowledge, or instructional repertoire. In some cases the teacher's problem frame is narrow, or potentially inaccurate or the range of strategies is limited. As a result, the supervisor shifts to the consulting stance. (See Nine Strategies for Learning-focused Consultation, p. 68).

### Functions

From the consulting stance, the supervisor clarifies standards by offering context specific examples to ensure that the teacher understands expectations. The consulting supervisor offers perspectives on present concerns, by naming possible causes and possible approaches to improve performance. Beyond this gap analysis, a thoughtful supervisor also shares essential information about learning and learners and curriculum and content as they relate to existing issues, principles of practice, connections to expected performance standards and relevant craft knowledge. By offering, *"Here's what you should pay attention to"* and *"Here's why that matters"* and *"Here are some options,"* learning-focused supervisors make their thinking transparent. As teachers internalize principles of learning and teaching, these understandings become resources for more generating their own approaches and solutions.

In planning for action, skillful supervisors propose a menu of teacher goals to promote student achievement and professional growth, and provide opportunities for the teacher to choose and prioritize. Defining indicators of success and confirming timelines for completion are essential parts of the planning process.

## Cautions

The verb to consult comes from the Latin 'consultare' meaning to give or take counsel. It is important to distinguish learning-focused consultation from simply fixing or telling. For many supervisors, the pressing needs they observe in classrooms triggers the impulse to help, by providing information and offering advice. While in the short-term this inclination may reduce the burdens of busy teachers or temporarily resolve an urgent issue, context-rich learning opportunities may be missed if advice is the only resource offered. Further, advice without explanation of the underlying choice points and guiding principles rarely develops teachers' abilities to transfer learning to new settings or to generate novel solutions on their own.

*[handwritten margin note: Just telling them is a temp fix — not a long term reflective internal approach that could help now & in the future]*

If overused, the consulting stance builds dependency on the supervisor for problem solving. Consultation that is learning-focused within a professional relationship offers the teacher both immediate support and the resources for tackling future problems with increasing independence, whatever that teacher's level of performance. Learning-focused supervisors do not allow their personal passion or organizational pressures to overcome patience with a teacher's developmental process.

---

### Consulting

Ms. Brighton, a second year teacher, has been reviewing the observation notes provided by her principal, Mr. Grayson, in anticipation of their reflecting conversation. He recently observed a seventh grade math lesson.

The data indicate that a third of the student responses to the practice problems at the end of the lesson were incomplete or incorrect. Mr. Grayson begins from a coaching stance, citing the data and asking, "What's your sense of what was happening for the students who were not successful?" Ms. Brighton considers this and suggests that these students may have been inattentive or confused during her explanations of the necessary math concepts.

Continuing from a coaching stance, Mr. Grayson inquires about formative assessment, and realizes that Ms. Brighton has limited repertoire in checking for students' understanding as a lesson progresses. As a result, there is little modification of instruction during her teaching. He decides to shift to a consulting stance.

"It is likely that your less successful students were confused early on. Consistently monitoring for student engagement and comprehension ensures that students have a good grasp of the building blocks before moving on. This practice is key to their learning success. One way you might do this is to pause and have students explain a key point to a partner and then randomly select several pairs to report. This pattern of pause, partner and survey increases your confidence and theirs that the fundamentals are in place as you continue or, if they are not, it allows you to modify your instruction to address any confusion before moving ahead. As we review plans for upcoming lessons, please think about and indicate some pause points for applying this pattern."

Ending the conversation from a coaching stance, Mr. Grayson asks Ms. Brighton to clarify her understanding and confirm next steps.

---

## Collaborating

In the collaborating stance the guiding question is, *"What are some ways to balance my contributions with this teacher's experiences and expertise?"*

The collaborative stance creates a shared platform for the co-construction of knowledge. In this stance, either participant can offer ideas, solutions, analysis, and so on. In many cases the learning-focused supervisor shifts to a collaborative stance to increase

*[handwritten margin note: graded release from sup to teacher, use this to get teacher more focused on what they need to do]*

Four Stances: The Continuum of Learning-focused Interaction

the teacher's confidence in his or her own ability to analyze data, frame problems, develop strategies. Much like the gradual release concept in classroom practice, it works towards greater ownership of the information and actions generated.

In this stance, the supervisor provides support for idea generation balanced with respect for the teacher's ability to generate ideas and solutions. A rich, inquiry-driven collaboration creates permission for the supervisor to add ideas and perspectives without dominating the conversation.

## Functions

From the collaborative stance, the supervisor and teacher jointly clarify standards to ensure shared understanding. Together, they use data to analyze gaps between expectations and current practice. In partnership, they analyze problems, generate potential causal theories, develop ideas and produce strategies for action. Shared perspectives lead to greater insights for both teacher and supervisor.

---

### Collaborating

Mr. Ruiz always looks forward to a lively engagement with Mr. Mathers after observing his tenth grade English class. Given the new curriculum, Mr. Mathers and his department colleagues are exploring strategies for increasing students' skill in assessing and revising their own written work. For this conversation, the principal and teacher each have a copy of the collected observational data as well as student writing samples to focus their reflection.

The unit objectives included students' ability to articulate, in writing, a persuasive argument supported by text-based evidence. During his observation, Mr. Ruiz noted students working as peer editors with the writing rubric between them, comparing their completed work to the standard. Mr. Mathers started the lesson with a review of the rubric and directed the students to use it to assess their essays. He rotated among the working groups during the class time. At the end of the period, he collected the edited work.

Mr. Ruiz begins the reflection from a coaching stance. Early in the conversation, he inquires about Mr. Mather's impressions of the collected student work. Mr. Mather's shares that the work was inconsistent and only a third of the students were able to clearly connect their own writing to a point on the rubric and use the standards to revise their work. As this was a new approach, he is not surprised by these results, but would like to figure out how to improve them and is uncertain about what specifically might have caused the lack of success.

Shifting to a collaborative stance, Mr. Ruiz suggests that they generate some potential causal factors. Based on their shared analyses, the list includes: poor choice of topic for this class, general gaps in written expression, lack of inferential reasoning skills, inability to incorporate text-based evidence, and a lack of clarity about the rubric itself.

Mr. Mathers considers this list, eliminating the skill-based causes based on his students' generally successful performance on previous written assignments. He determines that the most likely cause involves use of the rubric and peer editing as a learning approach, especially since both of these practices are new to him and his class.

As a result, Mr. Mathers proposes that his students could use more models of both the rubric and of strategies for peer editing. He decides to design a whole class lesson demonstrating editing and revision using the rubric. Mr. Ruiz chimes in with thoughts about guided practice using specific language that tenth graders might use so they feel confident correcting their peers.

Mr. Ruiz suggests, "Let's think about ways to monitor for students' success. What will you look for to know that this approach is working?" They continue generating ideas.

Concluding the conversation from a coaching stance, Mr. Ruiz asks, "What are some specific next steps you're taking away from this conversation?"

---

Each stance is in large part defined by which participant in the conversation is producing the information and/or analysis at a given moment. The collaborative stance has the widest range of participation. In this stance, both parties are contributing, however, the supervisor might lean more towards consulting by suggesting criteria or offering a principle of practice upon which to base the ideas. Or the supervisor might lead with a completely open-ended inquiry which leans more towards coaching.

## Cautions

To collaborate with integrity, supervisors need to resist their own impulses to dominate and provide the bulk of the analysis and thinking. It is important to purposefully invite and create a space for teacher contributions. Pausing to allow the teacher time to think and prompting and encouraging idea production communicates a belief in their personal and professional capacities.

*to create or come from teacher*

Learning-focused supervisors need to be especially careful to monitor for balance in the collaborative stance. Personal enthusiasm and interest in a topic, or a strong preference for a specific solution may override the intention to co-create ideas and actions. False collaboration then becomes disguised consultation or tacit calibration.

## Coaching

In the coaching stance the guiding question is, *"What mental and emotional resources might be most useful for this teacher at this time?"*

The coaching stance assumes that the teacher has the resources necessary to engage in data-centered reflection on practice and modify and manage personal learning. Operating from this stance conveys the supervisor's respect for the teacher's expertise and potential regarding these capacities.

## Functions

In the coaching stance, the supervisor references teaching and learning standards and a variety of data as focal points for the conversation. The supervisor inquires into the teacher's thinking about each of these resources as they relate to existing issues. In this stance, the teacher is the primary source of problem frames, gap analysis, potential solutions and strategies. Through an inquiry process, the supervisor's role is to enhance teacher's capacities for planning, reflecting, problem solving and decision-making. The coaching stance is one of inquiry. This means that there are multiple appropriate responses, and that the supervisor has not predetermined a correct answer.

The value of these questions is that they influence the teacher's underlying thought processes. By inquiring, pausing, and probing for details as data are explored, the supervisor supports both idea production and the exploration of the "whys" and "hows" of choices, possibilities, and connections. This nonjudgmental approach applied over time, enlarges the frame, developing the teacher's ever-increasing capacity for expert thinking and practice. The ultimate aim of the coaching stance is to develop a teacher's internal resources for self-coaching so that with time and practice, an increasingly sophisticated inner voice guides professional self-talk. In planning for action, supervisor questions guide the teacher's exploration of goals, success criteria and reasonable timelines for action.

## Cautions

In a coaching stance, supervisors reduce potential frustration by posing developmentally appropriate questions. These questions should stretch, not strain, thinking. Questions that require more knowledge or experience than is presently available to the teacher create anxiety and feelings of inadequacy. In such cases, it is more effective to offer information from a consultative stance and then shift to a coaching stance to explore that information.

Effective questions should invite teachers' thinking. The syntax and intonation of these inquiries welcomes multiple possible responses and does not signal that there is a preferred or correct answer. Supervisors should take care that their own preferences don't influence their listening or direct their questions.

### Coaching

With most of her staff, Dr. Salomon applies a coaching stance during post-observation conversations. This upcoming meeting regarding Ms. Mahoney's sixth grade class should be no exception.

After teaching eighth grade for many years, Ms. Mahoney has moved to sixth grade and is challenged by different developmental issues for these younger students. One of her goals is to establish a culture for learning in which students are highly engaged and self-directed towards high standards of performance.

Dr. Salomon is familiar with Ms. Mahoney's classroom having visited several times during the first weeks of school. This conversation involves a formal observation of a social studies lesson. She has sent ahead a copy of her observation notes along with some questions to think about. Ms. Mahoney, for her part, has recorded some of her own reflections about the lesson.

Dr. Salomon begins with an analysis question. "The data indicate that there was as much, or even more, student-to-student interaction about the topic as there was between you and the class. How does that compare to what you anticipated?" Ms. Mahoney shares that these basic interaction patterns are becoming more established, but that she's also focused on the quality of the student engagement. She draws the principal's attention to some of the student actions indicated in the data. She has already coded the observation notes for instances of peer support and praise and has noticed that of her 28 students, twelve exhibit these behaviors consistently, and many students don't do them at all.

Dr. Salomon invites her to explore some causal theories, "What's your hunch about what might be producing the positive behaviors?"

The conversation continues. Ms. Mahoney thoughtfully considers her practice as she responds to each inquiry. As a result, Dr. Salomon maintains a coaching stance throughout the conversation.

To conclude, Ms. Mahoney generates several new goals, and shares specific action steps for accomplishing them.

# The Continuum of Learning-focused Interaction

| | Calibrating | Consulting | Collaborating | Coaching |
|---|---|---|---|---|
| **Supervisor/Specialist** | **Information, analysis, goals** | | | |
| | | | **Information, analysis, goals** | **Teacher** |
| **Guiding question** | What are the gaps/growth areas indicated for this teacher based on present performance levels and the standards? | What information, ideas and technical resources will be most useful to this teacher at this time? | What are some ways to balance my contributions with this teacher's experiences and expertise? | What mental and emotional resources might be most useful for this teacher at this time? |
| **Function** | • Articulating standards<br>• Using data to identify gaps between expected standards and present results<br>• Defining problems<br>• Prescribing results | • Clarifying standards<br>• Using data to analyze gaps between expected standards and present results<br>• Offering information and ideas<br>• Providing problem analysis and perspectives<br>• Naming principles of practice | • Jointly clarifying standards<br>• Using data to co-analyze gaps between expected standards and present results<br>• Co-generating information and ideas<br>• Co-analyzing problems<br>• Expanding perspectives | • Referencing standards as a focal point<br>• Using data to explore gaps between expected standards and present results<br>• Facilitating teacher idea production<br>• Mediating teacher problem-framing and analysis<br>• Enhancing teacher capacities for planning, reflecting, problem-solving and decision making |
| **Role in planning for action** | • Determining teacher actions/goal<br>• Naming success criteria<br>• Establishing timelines | | • Co-constructing teacher actions/goals<br>• Co-developing success criteria<br>• Agreeing on timelines | • Exploring teacher actions/goals<br>• Eliciting success criteria<br>• Clarifying timelines |
| **Cues** | • Credible voice<br>• Using neutral language, as in "These data ..." "This example ..." | | • Approachable voice<br>• Collective pronouns, as in "Let's think about ..." "How might we ..." | • Approachable voice<br>• Second person pronouns, as in "What are some of your ...?" "How might you...?" |
| **Cautions** | • Take care not to let personal preferences become prescription Judgments must be supported by clear, external criteria.<br>• Use literal observation notes, classroom artifacts and assessment data to avoid subjectivity or bias. | ... to help or don't let ... personal passion overcome patience with the developmental process.<br>• Be aware that overuse of the consulting stance may build dependency on the supervisor for problem solving. | • Resist the impulse to dominate the conversation and provide the bulk of the analysis and thinking.<br>• Monitor for balance in idea production. Don't allow personal enthusiasm or preferences to override the intention to co-create ideas and options. | • Reduce potential frustration by posing developmentally appropriate questions. Questions should stretch not strain thinking.<br>• Be sure that questions allow for multiple responses and do not signal that there is a preferred answer. |

*(handwritten notes: "Teacher has to take ownership! We should not be driving ownership" and "Inquiry based open ended")*

Four Stances: The Continuum of Learning-focused Interaction

## Navigating Strategically

Except for calibrating, stance is not predetermined and best practice suggests both entering the conversation from a coaching stance with an initial inquiry and ending the conversation with an inquiry to clarify next steps. Both supervisors and teachers must be clear that the intention of the supervisory process is to support learning and growth. Without this clarity, a potential "learning moment" might be lost, or the teacher might misinterpret the supervisor's intent.

The calibrating stance is unique in that it focuses on what needs to be learned; that is, it names gaps between present practice and expected standards. This stance does not produce the learning, it names the learning targets for the teacher.

Once learning goals have been established, flexible supervisors navigate strategically across the continuum, choosing the most appropriate stances for promoting a teacher's growth.

## Establishing the Third Point

Skilled supervisors establish a clear focus for the conversation, a third point. In learning-focused supervision, a lesson plan or data and a standards-based scale with levels of performance serve as effective third points. The third point shifts the cognitive and emotional energy from the supervisor/teacher relationship to the data. Effective use of a third point includes both verbal and nonverbal elements: a physical shift from face-to-face to eyes on the data; physical reference to the data source with a still hand, or frozen gesture; and neutral pronouns when referring to the data, for example: the observations, these results, this student work.

Learning-focused supervisors facilitate thinking from any stance. Skillful supervisors intentionally guide the teacher's experience, through questions, highlights and references. Supervisors also use emphasis to clarify their purpose and importance, to sort significant principles or patterns from less significant details, and to create opportunities for their teachers to build and construct understanding.

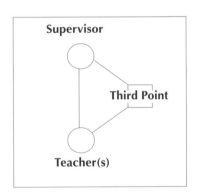

Imagine, for instance, a supervisor and teacher are exploring post-observation data. They are focusing on the standards for instruction and reviewing the supervisor's script of the teacher's questions. The supervisor offers the following question:

Supervisor: *"As you look at the script of your questions during this lesson, what are some comparisons you're making between your choices and the rubric description for Using Questions and Discussion Techniques?"*

Teacher: *"I noticed that for three of the questions, there was practically no wait time and many of the questions were recall. But, those are the kinds of questions my students can answer."*

At this point, the supervisor might take a consulting stance, sharing some principles of practice related to teacher questions and promoting student thinking, offering a menu of ways to scaffold for greater student success. She might then use a similar pattern exploring other observational data related to standards for instruction. In this way the teacher has several concrete examples that clarify and calibrate to the standards, as well as a model for a more sophisticated lens for examining her own practice. As they continue the conversation, the supervisor might then shift to a collaborative stance, suggesting that they brainstorm ideas for challenging student thinking.

## Four Stances: The Continuum of Learning-focused Interaction

**Using the Third Point**

*"The data indicate . . . "*

*"Given these behaviors, it is likely that these students . . . "*

*"Based on these results, next steps need to be . . . "*

## Mediating Nonverbally

Physically referencing the third point in a space off to the side between the parties provides a psychologically safe place for information, concerns and problems. This careful use of space and gesture depersonalizes ideas. It is now not the supervisor's information or problem, the teacher's information or problem or even 'our' information or problem. It is simply information or a problem about which and with which to think. Information placed as a third point frees the teacher to accept, modify or reject the idea as an idea – not connected to personalities. Thus, placement of the conversational focus creates a triangle, either literally or referentially, keeping the conversational container psychologically safe. Without this subtle, but critical distancing, the teacher might feel trapped in a web of relationship and have difficulty freely accepting or rejecting an idea, for fear of hurt feelings or repercussion.

Nonverbal tools, such as posture, gesture and voice tone are all indicators of the stance we are taking. In a calibrating stance, physical and visual focus should be on the third point documents. While referencing the documents with a frozen gesture, speak with a credible voice using neutral language such as *"the* standard", *"this* domain", *"the* results" to articulate expectations and performance gaps. The intention is to make standards and performance metrics the authority and not set up a power struggle between supervisor and teacher.

In a consulting stance, the third point information or referential space focuses the conversations on information and ideas and not on the supervisor or the teacher. Here again, the credible voice conveys the tonality of wisdom and experience. At times it may be appropriate to use personal pronouns as in, "Here's how *I've* learned to think about issues like this." or, "In *my* experience is often works best to..." The possible danger is that some teachers upon hearing the personal pronoun will respond to it as a command and not a suggestion. When in doubt use neutral language such as, "Best practices suggest that..." or, "Other teachers with this dilemma have had success with...."

In a collaborating stance supervisor and teacher are operating both physically and metaphorically side-by-side, dividing their attention between the third point information and each other. The supervisor's voice tone is collegial and approachably confident using inclusive pronouns such as *"Let's* think about this..." or, *"We* might want to start by..." or, *"Our"* next step might be to..."

In a coaching stance, the third point information is a catalyst for idea generation and problem solving by the teacher. There tends to be greater eye contact between the teacher and supervisor who uses a more rhythmic and approachable voice modulation to create a safe space for thought and reflection. The dominant pronoun is "you", as in "So *you're* noticing some patterns in your classroom routines that seem to be working." or, "What are some ways *you're* thinking about increasing student engagement in *your* next math lesson?"

Because learning-focused supervision is standards-driven and data-based, the use of a third point is especially important in the calibrating and consulting stances. Physically referencing the third point depersonalizes delivery of any information or judgment. It creates a "thing" to which the teacher can attach emotional reactions. By purposefully establishing a third point, the supervisor transforms a potential confrontation into an opportunity to provide clear feedback. By reducing the perception of personal attack, the feedback becomes information that can be heard and applied.

**Third Point Examples**

Observational data

Samples of student work

Rubrics

Lesson plans

Standards (content, student work or effective teaching)

Test results or other performance data

Four Stances: The Continuum of Learning-focused Interaction

## Choosing Stance

Skillful supervisors attend to the signals of the teachers with whom they are interacting to determine their choice of learning-focused stance. By attending to the teacher's verbal and nonverbal behaviors as they generate ideas and respond to inquiries, the aware supervisor can assess the effectiveness of a given stance and know whether and when to move along the continuum.

### During Learning-focused Conversations, skillful supervisors attend to:

The depth of content knowledge and pedagogy:

- How well does the teacher understand the knowledge, skills and concepts being explored by the lesson or unit being considered?
- To what degree does the teacher understand the connections between ideas in the curriculum?
- To what degree does the teacher understand and remember what came before and what follows a specific lesson?

The level of knowledge the teacher has about the students and their learning needs:

- Does the teacher describe the students in terms of their strengths and limitations to learning? Can the teacher articulate how the demographics represented in the class have influenced the planning?
- In what ways has the teacher made planning decisions based on individual students' learning styles, language abilities, cultural differences, or possible limitations?

The teacher's ability to select instructional outcomes for short and long-range student learning:

- Do the teacher's goals depend solely on external sources such as the teachers' guide, or do they display the teacher's customization based on knowledge of the students and the content? How thoroughly does the teacher explain how the outcomes were selected?
- Does the teacher state the goals/outcomes in terms of student learning rather than activities?
- Does the teacher articulate both a short-range view of outcomes and long-range targets for problem solving skills and higher-level thinking?
- Does the teacher explain how the lesson connects to other lessons and larger contexts?

The depth of knowledge of a range of resources:

- How does the teacher plan to use the resources provided by the school, and those available through other sources?
- Does the teacher use resources for increasing personal expertise in either the content or pedagogy for this lesson?

What the teacher's language reveals about the coherent design of the instruction:

- What information does the teacher give about the details and level of sophistication of the intended strategies?
- How extensive and with what degree of nuance does the teacher understand the strategies to be employed?
- Is a given strategy option the only piece of repertoire, or was it selected strategically from a group of choices?
- Does the plan include considerations of appropriate sequencing of learning activities and a balance of learning styles?

The nature of the teacher's plan for formative and summative assessment:

- How does the teacher intend to determine if the learning goals are met? Is the teacher clear on the success criteria?
- Are the intended assessments congruent with the planned outcomes?
- What are the teacher's intentions for using the assessment data, either during the lesson, or in future planning?

## Versatility Matters

Expert supervision requires a repertoire of knowledge and skills for engaging teachers in productive formal and informal conversations. These professional resources provide the foundation for operating along the Continuum as we interact with colleagues. Having access to one's repertoire opens up possibilities for successful learning-focused experiences and offers options for consideration when a given approach is not working. Knowing what we know and don't know helps us to identify gaps in our repertoire so we can consciously expand our own capacities as growth agents.

Versatility matters. In any given conversation, any one of the four stances may be appropriate. By reading the verbal and nonverbal cues of the colleague with whom we are engaged and responding accordingly, we can then flex along the continuum to support learning and growth. This flexibility in stance is the key to successful supervisory relationships. If our goal is to increase teachers' capacities for self-direction, we need to continually offer opportunities to think, reflect and problem-solve within the flow of the real work of learning to teach. Our ability to continually anticipate, monitor and flex our stance across the Continuum of Interaction is a vital component in developing and maintaining learning-focused supervisory relationships.

Four Stances: The Continuum of Learning-focused Interaction

# 3. Structured Conversations

Applying a shared and agreed upon structure to our conversations maximizes time, and also serves to focus attention by providing a scaffold for supporting and challenging thinking within a specified context. For example, when a supervisor and teacher schedule planning or reflecting conversations, a structure for guiding the interaction offers topical focus and permission to keep the conversation moving. A structure designed for planning increases rigor by highlighting the cognitive outcomes that support effective planning, such as predicting, envisioning and forecasting. A structure designed for reflection increases rigor by highlighting the cognitive outcomes that support effective reflection, such as recollection, cause-effect reasoning and generalizing. With consistent application, a conversation structure sets expectations for high engagement, complex thinking and no surprises or "gotchas".

The conversation templates on the following pages are samples of efficient guides for purposeful interactions. They are based on fundamental and current theories of learning (see, for example, Bransford, Brown & Cocking, 1999; Marzano, Pickering & Pollack, 2001; Hattie 2009) that suggest the importance of specific intentions within a learning-focused interaction. The general templates are based on the three phases in the Pathways Learning Model (Lipton & Wellman, 2000).

Each phase on the template serves a specific purpose. The Activating and Engaging phase establishes context and frames of reference. It activates prior knowledge and experience, surfacing the orientation and perception of the teacher regarding the topic at hand. It engages relationship, as well as mental and emotional awareness, and sets the scene for a thoughtful, learning-focused conversation. The Exploring and Discovering phase, whether in planning or reflecting, provides an opportunity for examining the details of specific events, making inferences and analyzing experiences; while the Organizing and Integrating phase supports generalizing from these explorations and bringing new learning forward.

The general template can be tailored for specific purposes. The Planning Template that follows supports effective thinking about lesson and unit design. Its counterpart, the Reflecting Template, is designed to elicit thoughtful reflection and produce transfer from one experience to many. Notice that these templates are designed to direct attention and focus on particular cognitive outcomes. For example, when planning, the supervisor's paraphrasing and inquiry should cause the planner to predict, envision, and describe. While reflecting, the skillful supervisor guides analysis, cause-effect reasoning and synthesis. Each of these structures guides thinking and produces inferences, hypotheses and new connections.

Flexibility in stance is an integral part of applying the conversation templates on the pages that follow. While the questions are framed from a coaching stance, learning-focused supervisors shift stances to support the teacher in producing the information and thinking processes within each phase of the template. For example, from a calibrating stance within a planning conversation, the approach might include naming specific lesson goals linked to standards drawn from the content area of that lesson and naming explicit success criteria. Within a consulting stance, the supervisor might offer a menu of possible goals from which the teacher can choose, modify or adapt. As a consultant, the

# Learning-focused Conversations   A Template for **Planning**

## ACTIVATING AND ENGAGING

### CONTEXT
- What are some things about your students' readiness (social skills, routines, self-management) that are influencing your lesson (unit) design?
- What are some of the skills/ knowledge students will need to bring to this lesson (unit) to be successful?

### PRESENTING ISSUES
- What are some special areas/ student needs you will need to address?
- What are some issues you anticipate might influence student learning?

## EXPLORING AND DISCOVERING

### GOALS AND OUTCOMES
- As you think about what you know about your students, and the content, what are some key learning goals?
- What are some ways that these goals integrate with other content learning?
- What are some thinking skills students will need to apply?

### INDICATORS OF SUCCESS
- Given these goals, what are some things you expect to see/hear as students are achieving them?
- Given these goals, how will you monitor student learning?
- What kinds of assessments will you use to determine student success?

### APPROACHES, STRATEGIES AND RESOURCES
- What are some strategies you're planning that will both challenge students and support their success?
- What are some ways you'll ensure high engagement for all students?
- What are some resources or materials you/your students will need to support and extend student learning?

### POTENTIAL CHOICE POINTS AND CONCERNS
- As you anticipate teaching the lesson, what are some points where students might struggle?
- What are some options for supporting struggling students and enriching those who need greater challenge?
- Should you notice that students' attention is drifting, what are some possibilities for reengaging them?

## ORGANIZING AND INTEGRATING

### PERSONAL LEARNING
- What are some ways that this lesson provides opportunities to pursue your own learning goals?
- What new learning/skills will you try or exercise in this lesson?

### NEXT STEPS
- As a result of this conversation, what are some next steps?

# Learning-focused Conversations   A Template for **Reflecting**

## ACTIVATING AND ENGAGING

RECOLLECTIONS
- As you reflect on this lesson/unit, what are some things that come to mind?
- Given your recollections, what are some things that captured your attention?

PERSPECTIVES AND PERCEPTIONS
- In this lesson/unit, what was particularly satisfying?
- In this lesson/unit, what were some things that concerned you?

## EXPLORING AND DISCOVERING

WEIGHING EVIDENCE
- What is some of the evidence that supports your impressions/ judgments?
- What are some examples that stand out for you (student responses, work samples, interaction patterns)?

SEARCH FOR PATTERNS
- Given what occurred, how typical are these results?
- What percentage of the time does this (behavior, learning, response pattern . . .) tend to happen?

COMPARE/CONTRAST
- How similar or different is what you anticipated from what occurred?
- How might you compare students who were successful to those who were less so?

ANALYZE CAUSE-EFFECT
- What are some factors that influenced what happened?
- Given (specific success/concern), what's your hunch about what may have it produced it?

## ORGANIZING AND INTEGRATING

GENERALIZATIONS
- What are some big ideas that you are taking away from this conversation?
- Based on this experience, what are some new connections (about students, curriculum, instruction) that you are making?

APPLICATIONS
- What are some things that you are taking away from this experience that will influence your practice in the future?
- As a result of new learning, what are some goals you're setting (for yourself, for your students, curriculum, this unit)?

supervisor might also offer some possible success indicators for those goals. In a reflecting conversation, the supervisor might encourage a collaborative stance and join the teacher in brainstorming a list of possible cause-effect connections between what occurred and the approaches and actions upon which the teacher is reflecting.

## Planning Conversations

Planning conversations offer fundamental learning opportunities for modeling and extending the intellectual habits of goal-driven thinking. Effective teachers set clear goals for their instruction, and identify specific systems for monitoring their achievement. They also generate contingencies should their initial planning prove unsuccessful during implementation. Attention to planning, and understanding the ways in which experts think about their plans, is especially important to the development of novice and low-performing teachers. Applying the template helps internalize important planning questions teachers must consider to produce high achievement for their students. These questions explore key components such as learning outcomes, student learning needs, instructional design and assessment. Doing so with the support of a supervisor increases a teacher's confidence and capacity for effective, independent instructional planning.

In the Activating and Engaging phase, establishing the context for the lesson or event allows the supervisor and teacher to "get in the room together", both the immediate space of moment-to-moment rapport and the conceptual space of the teacher's classroom. Experienced supervisors preserve time for more elaborative thinking in the Exploring and Discovering phase by moving through this first phase as efficiently as possible.

The second phase, Exploring and Discovering, is where the bulk of the time is spent in a typical planning conversation. The four focus arenas are arranged in order of priority. This is especially important to emphasize to novice and low performing teachers, who tend to spend more of their time designing activities and approaches, and less of their time clarifying goals and success indicators. Reducing activity-driven planning is an important goal for learning-focused supervisors. Teacher thinking is supported and enhanced through questions that reveal their knowledge and application of essential planning and preparation components.

The third phase, Organizing and Integrating, emerges from the general flow of the conversation. The two focus arenas in this phase of the template offer options for extending and solidifying awareness and clarifying next steps. Over time, skillful supervisors note potential stretch arenas for their teachers and select focusing questions and/or suggestions within these arenas accordingly.

In addition, lesson planning is an important opportunity for supervisors to support the development of a teacher's thinking capacities (Clark and Peterson, 1986). By encouraging detailed planning that explores choice points and monitoring strategies, supervisors help novices develop the habits of mind of more skilled practitioners. For example, by observing and participating in a teacher's planning, supervisors gain insight into mental processes and can develop tailored strategies to support and extend thinking in this area.

By noting where in the planning process a teacher needs the most support, a skilled supervisor can decide when and how to move from coaching to consulting during a given conversation. Structured planning conversations also offer a supervisor insight into how the teacher thinks about teaching and learning. Important knowledge, such

Structured Conversations

as understanding student needs, curriculum, and content related to key skills, such as determining learning outcomes, designing cohesive instruction and creating formative assessments are all topics for an effective planning conversation. The exchange allows the supervisor to note general patterns of thought for this teacher and know when to support, and when and how to challenge this individual.

## Specialized Applications for the Planning Conversation Template

We propose the conversation templates as frameworks and not as recipes to be followed in a step-by-step fashion. The questions within each phase beneath each focus arena are intended as models and possibilities; not as the only options. Different conversations will take on different flavors. Although these templates are relatively generic, thoughtful attention to their use for specialized functions produces powerful results.

### Problem Solving Conversations

The Planning Template is also a useful scaffold for supporting problem solving. Hallmarks of an expert problem solver include the ability to envision the desired state and specify the outcomes of a viable solution. Skillful problem solvers can also articulate criteria for and indicators of success. The Planning Template is designed to pursue these topics as they relate to the teacher's specific concerns. Again, learning-focused supervisors can apply one or several stances to the problem solving conversation, balancing support with challenge as they do so.

### Goal-Setting Conversations

The Planning Conversation Template is a natural scaffold for goal-setting. During Activating and Engaging, the teacher shares initial impressions about the data. The supervisor and teacher then examine and analyze these data for gaps and gains during Exploring and Discovering. As the conversation progresses, supervisor and teacher develop clear and measurable goals. Ultimately, while Organizing and Integrating, they agree upon next steps for action based on the newly developed professional goals.

During the Activating and Engaging phase in a goal-setting conversation, it is important to take some time to clarify the roles, responsibilities and options available for both supervisor and teacher. Defining the supervisor's role initiates a partnership which can be shaped and negotiated to serve the learning needs of both members. Discussing the expectations of each partner reduces the possibility of disappointment or miscommunication down the road. Sharing information about the four stances makes it possible for a teacher to request a certain type of interaction, depending on needs.

Use the Exploring and Discovering phase to establish clear goals for the supervisor-teacher relationship, as well. Further, when a teacher clearly articulates his or her own learning goals, the supervisor can focus energy and resource on supporting the teacher in achieving them. Both types of clear, concrete and specific goal setting are important to the learning-focused relationship. The Planning Template is an effective structure for guiding these initial goal-setting conversations.

During the Organizing and Integrating phase, complete the goal-setting conversation by having the teacher summarize his or her understandings and name the next steps.

## Reflecting Conversations

Data-based reflecting conversations consolidate and extend professional thinking and habits of mind. They typically occur after lesson observations, or at scheduled intervals to reflect upon patterns of teaching practice and student learning. Reflecting Conversations are especially useful at transition points in the curriculum, when unit topics switch; or at significant points in the school year, such as the close of marking periods. The use of literal data, such as classroom observation scripts, rubric-based analysis and student work products grounds the conversation by providing concrete evidence of the outcome of planned actions.

Here again, the Activating and Engaging phase matters greatly. The teacher's issues and concerns and/or perspectives and perceptions are important to surface. Depending upon what emerges, the skilled supervisor will select a stance to explore the teacher's current awareness. For example, if the teacher notes some issues of concern and not others that the supervisor deems equally important, the supervisor as calibrator or consultant may add these to the list of topics to explore during the Exploring and Discovering phase.

Reflecting on data with the teacher after lessons have been taught, supervisors support the re-examination of earlier thinking and help teachers make connections as they analyze successes and review shortcomings.

During the Exploring and Discovering phase, asking the teacher to weigh priorities is not only a respectful approach; but also provides a contextually sound assessment of the ways in which this teacher is developing as a professional. Experts notice more than novices. By noting what the teacher is noticing and about what the teacher is concerned, the aware supervisor can select an appropriate stance and help frame the content for reflection.

During the Organizing and Integrating phase, experienced supervisors widen the conversation from immediate issues to the bigger picture. The connection making, generalizations, applications and personal learnings that emerge at this phase increase the likelihood of transfer of new awareness and insight. This is the true test of learning-focused conversations. Building habits of reflection and supporting transfer of and applications of learning is a critical responsibility for supervisors.

Creating reflective, self-directed practitioners is an important aspect of the supervisor-teacher relationship. Formal, structured opportunities to do so make a powerful contribution to developing this disposition. Note that the Reflecting Template is designed to elicit personal discoveries, as well as new learning about teaching practice.

## Navigating Within and Across the Conversation Templates

We offer a metaphor of 'map' for the Conversation Templates. A map defines boundaries, clarifying what belongs inside and what is external to the territory. So, too, do these structures provide clarity about the parameters of the conversation. In this way, when used skillfully, they are especially time efficient, allowing either colleague to return to the agreed upon purpose(s) of the meeting. A map also can be shared, so both parties know what territory can be explored and what routes are possible—whether we take the same path each time, or vary it. Further, while each area on a map is clearly defined, we may choose to apportion our time visiting several neighborhoods, or spend most of it concentrated in one or two. In fact, once the supervisor and teacher have had some

## Structured Conversations

experience with the Conversation Templates, they are rarely applied linearly. That is, moving from one arena (establishing goals and outcomes) to another (potential choice points) and then to a third (indicators of success) and then back to the first (for more goals and outcomes) is quite common. It also makes sense, frequently, to navigate across the templates. In this case, the supervisor and teacher reflect on past experiences during a planning conversation, or finish a reflecting conversation with questions for applying new learning to a future plan.

The Planning and Reflecting Templates offer a structure to supervisor-teacher conversations. These guides enhance the efficiency of meeting time by providing a shared focus. They also serve as learning scaffolds, encouraging teachers to internalize the thinking protocols that guide effective planning and reflection about their own practice. The questions and ways of thinking that are explored during structured conversations become an internal voice for self-directed growth.

As a result, after several cycles of planning, observation and reflection using the Conversation Templates, the teacher comes to a planning or reflecting meeting prepared to respond to the challenging questions of the supervisor. This readiness and confidence sets the stage for increasingly rigorous conversations about teaching practice and increasingly effective solutions to the inevitable challenges of classroom life.

# 4. A Learning-focused Toolkit

Effective communication is respectful and reciprocal. Learning-focused conversations require supervisors and teachers to listen and speak in equal measure so that each party can be heard and can influence the thinking of the other. However, what supervisors say is not always what teachers hear. Effective supervisory conversations create awareness and shared understanding. To engage in these conversations, supervisors make skillful use of a learning-focused toolkit that includes both non-verbal and verbal tools.

Like any collection of tools, these can be used with differing degrees of skill, need regular sharpening, and contain specialty items for specific purposes. These purposes include: building productive working relationships, supporting continuous learning and encouraging commitment to action. By listening carefully to their teachers, growth-promoting supervisors tailor their responses to increase receptivity and stimulate thinking.

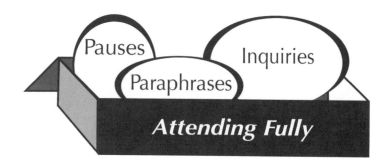

The learning-focused toolkit presented in this chapter includes physical alignment, listening, pausing, paraphrasing and inquiring. This toolkit operates in concert with the The Continuum of Learning-focused Interaction (see Chapter 2) and focuses on the templates for planning and reflecting (See Chapter 3). Being fully present is fundamental for applying these tools.

## Being Present

Given the many demands of life in schools, being fully present with others is often a challenge for busy supervisors. Focusing complete attention on another person requires emotional and mental discipline to shut out both external and internal distractions. We cannot fake listening. As a species we have developed finely regulated systems for assessing and detecting when other people are paying attention to us. Babies learn to recognize and regulate their feelings based on their parents' reactions to their vocalizations, facial expressions and other physical behaviors. Psychologists refer to this process as attunement. Well-attuned parents detect and reflect the baby's responses, creating a feedback loop that shapes the developing brain and the parent-infant bond. We carry this system of awareness within us as adults. Learning-focused conversations tap these resources when attentive supervisors align with and focus their energy on the teachers with whom they are interacting.

### Threat Detection

The human brain is wired for threat detection. We rapidly assess information in our environment for signs of danger. These signals, whether real or imagined, are fast tracked on the brain's neural superhighways, taking priority over other, more thoughtful processes. Incoming signals from visual, auditory and tactile circuits flow into the amygdala, an almond shaped structure located deep within the limbic system in the midbrain. The amygdala's essential task is to connect emotional content to memory. This works for both positive and negative emotional experiences. The cortex, which holds higher level thinking structures, has more circuits running from the amygdala than the reverse.

Biologically, emotions drive thinking and attention, helping us to create meaning. For conversations to be learning-focused the teacher has to feel safe not to know --- thinking out loud is risk-taking. When the perception of threat emerges in a supervisory conversation it comes when the teacher's amygdala makes a rapid assessment of the body language, facial expressions, voice tone and language choices of the supervisor. The molecules of emotion then swiftly hijack the brain/body system. The impression of threat inhibits thinking processes causing the teacher to "shut down" and revert to survival mode: freeze, fight or flight.

## Communicating Our Attention

At the most basic level we signal our full attention nonverbally by aligning with the other person. Alignment has three distinct categories: physical, vocal and breathing patterns.

### Physical

Physical elements include muscle tension, posture and gesture. People who are aligned adopt similar postures with matching muscle tensions, reflecting or "borrowing" gestures from each other. Imagine you are in a restaurant, observing two people across the room. You can tell if they are relating well, even if you can't hear what they are saying. You might observe them leaning in towards each other, nodding, smiling, and gesturing animatedly as they engage in conversation. They dance the dance of attunement as the talk shifts back and forth.

Attentive supervisors physically align their bodies with the teacher by sitting at ninety-degree angle, ideally at the corner of a table, matching posture and physically "paraphrasing" the teacher's gestures. Physical barriers such as having a desk between the supervisor and teacher tend to interfere with alignment, creating both physical and emotional distance and may produce anxiety in the teacher.

### Vocal

Vocal elements include intonation, pacing and word choice. Humans are wired to appropriate the vocal patterns of those around them. In close proximity, we develop shared accents, speech patterns and vocabularies. When traveling to other parts of the country we tend to notice the vocal patterns of the natives, especially when these are different from our home region. This same type of vocal alignment occurs within professions when practitioners develop and use lexicons and jargons.

By consciously noting and pacing the patterns of others, adept supervisors first match and then modulate the conversation to connect emotionally and increase understanding. The supervisor can then carefully adjust the tone, pace and language of the conversation to increase thoughtfulness and increase learning opportunities.

## Breathing Patterns

Breathing patterns include depth, duration and rate. When humans align, they match breathing patterns. This occurs across the range of human emotions. We breathe shallowly and fast when we are upset and more deeply and slowly when relaxed. These respiration patterns are linked to muscle tension as a part of the physical systems linked to emotional responses. A common experience for parents when reading at bedtime is to unconsciously match the breathing pattern of the child, and as the little one nods off the parent too gets increasingly drowsy.

Learning-focused supervisors note the breathing patterns of teachers with whom they are interacting. Matching posture and muscle tension tends to produce a match in depth, duration and rate of breathing. Thinking brains consume a great deal of oxygen. Deeper breathing produces the needed energy for these processes.

## Attunement and Alignment

To engage fully in thoughtful and sometimes difficult explorations of teaching and learning issues, teachers have to be able to draw upon physical and emotional resources. Supervisors need to anticipate when they need to be especially attentive of the need for attunement and alignment. These occasions include times when:

- We anticipate tension or anxiety or when tension or anxiety emerges within the conversation. For example, no matter how positive the relationship between a supervisor and teacher, there is likely to be some anxiety when we engage in a reflecting conversation about a classroom observation or when reviewing a lesson plan together.

- We are having difficulty understanding another person. Sometimes it feels like we're operating on different wavelengths. When miscommunication occurs, purposeful realignment and matching a colleague physically is often an effective strategy for reengaging and increasing comprehension of the other person's ideas.

- We are distracted or having difficulty paying attention. So often, the limited time we have to meet with a teacher is "borrowed" from time we would devote to other tasks. Sometimes it is difficult to keep these tasks, both personal and professional, from diverting us from the conversation. In such cases, intentional monitoring for alignment keeps our attention fully on our colleague.

**Attunement and alignment matter most when:**

- we anticipate tension or anxiety or when tension or anxiety emerges within the conversation

- we are having difficulty understanding

- we are distracted or having difficulty paying attention

## Listening to Understand

Attentive listening is a full body experience, requiring our complete focus on the other person and noticing and managing any inner responses which may be distracting us from the information and meaning that the other person is trying to convey. The English word listen has roots associated with the words ear and to lean or list. When listening carefully, we literally give ear to another by listing or leaning physically and emotionally in the direction of the speaker.

Listening without formulating internal judgments and responses takes practice and discipline. The normal speaking rate is about 125-150 words per minute (Waks, 2010). Estimates of listening rates vary from 500 to 800 words per-minute, meaning that humans can process speech at a higher rate than speakers produce it. Most listeners fill this gap between speaking rate and processing rate with their own thoughts and judgments and in

doing so may miss essential information about the speaker's ideas, emotions and current degree of understanding of the issues being considered.

## Three Blocks to Understanding

There are three common internal distractions to effective listening. These blocks to understanding shift our listening focus inward, to our own opinion, interests or surety about a solution. This shift to 'I' diminishes understanding. For learning-focused supervisors it is particularly important to maintain awareness and listening discipline. Listening from our own world-view diminishes our capacity to understand a teacher's perceptions and concerns.

Descriptions of three specific categories of 'I' listening: personal listening, detail listening, and certainty listening follow. Learning-focused supervision is 'other-minded'. In many ways the listening limitations, or blocks to understanding, are 'self-ish' forms of listening, with a focus inwardly on our self and not outwardly on our conversation partner.

**Blocks to Understanding**

- Personal listening
- Detail listening
- Certainty listening

### Personal listening

Personal listening inspires *'me too'* or *'I would never'* responses, whether internally or spoken aloud. It occurs when our minds shift from listening to understand another to considering what is being said with reference to our own experiences and then judging its worth. Personal listening often leads to judgmental responses or personal anecdotes. Brief examples from the supervisor's own experiences may be appropriate to build the relationship and show empathy. However, there is a fine line between those intentions and the supervisor's story or personal perspective becoming the focus of the conversation.

When personal listening, the potential message to the teacher is that the supervisor's perspective, experience and knowledge is more important than the teacher's thinking.

### Detail listening

Detail listening drives our attention when we are concerned that the specifics might not be in place, and we inquire to ensure that they are. This listening may be triggered when the supervisor feels the need to have the complete picture in order to support the teacher. For example, detail listening produces questions like, *"What type of container will you use for each group's art supplies?"* These questions tend to stimulate recall of inconsequential information, rather than lead to more complex thinking.

When detail listening, the potential message to the teacher is one of mistrust that the important logistics are in place, or may be overlooked unless the supervisor inquires about them.

### Certainty listening

Certainty listening occurs when we are sure we know the solution to the problem, sometimes before we've listened carefully enough to be sure that we understand the teacher's perception about a problem. Before an issue is fully framed and mutually understood, this type of listening motivates us to offer advice, or inauthentic inquiries like *"Have you tried . . .?"* or *"Have you thought about . . .?"* Queries of this type are forms of disguised advice and typically do not inspire thoughtfulness on the part of teachers.

A Learning-focused Toolkit

When certainty listening, the potential message to the teacher is that the supervisor has greater knowledge and expertise about the issue at hand, or that the supervisor's way is the 'right' way.

Giving our full attention to a colleague contributes to relationship and to clear communication. These are the foundations for mutual learning and future exploration. Relationship and learning are intertwined both in-the-moment and over time. Learning and thinking draw upon person-to-person and person-to-idea connections. Subtle moves and behaviors nurture these relationships and desired thinking processes. Our consciousness of these components helps us to support productive outcomes. Inattention to these elements can hinder or block interpersonal and intellectual connection-making.

## Pacing for Thoughtfulness: Using Purposeful Pauses

In our time-conscious culture, fast-paced conversations coupled with a lack of focused attention undermine teachers' capacities for and confidence in their abilities to think energetically about the work of learning and teaching. Some people erroneously equate speed of response with higher degrees of intelligence. When supervisors make this mistake and do not adjust their pace to the thinking pace of the teacher with whom they are engaging they may cut off developing thoughts or prematurely jump to a consulting stance in an attempt to rescue their "struggling" colleague.

The pace of a conversation affects both the emotional and intellectual climate. Frequent, well-placed pauses create and support a climate for thinking. For most people, however, consciously pausing to provide a space for this thinking requires patience and practice. Silence can feel uncomfortable for both the listener and speaker unless there is a shared understanding that complex thinking takes and requires time.

## Purposeful Pausing

Supervisors support teacher thinking when they strategically pause during learning-focused conversations. Science educator and researcher Mary Budd Rowe (1986) first noted the positive effects of pausing in the classroom. She labeled these pauses Wait Time. Wait Time is the length of time we pause to allow thinking. Rowe suggests three to five seconds. Higher-level cognitive tasks may require a full five seconds or more.

In supervisory conversations, there are four critical junctures for pausing: after asking a question, after the teacher has offered initial thinking, before paraphrasing and after a paraphrase.

- Pause after asking a question. This pause allows time and signals support for thinking. It communicates our belief in the teacher's capacity and willingness to think.
- Pause after the teacher has offered initial thinking. This pause allows the teacher to mentally retrieve additional and/ or related information.
- Pause before paraphrasing. This pause allows the supervisor to fully absorb the teacher's communication and to construct an appropriate paraphrase.
- Pause after a paraphrase. This pause allows the teacher to confirm or correct the paraphrase and allows the supervisor to consider a strategic next move. Options include asking a question to move forward on the conversation template, to go deeper within the area being explored, to inquire for detail or to shift to another stance on the Continuum.

**Four Types of Pauses**

- Pause after asking a question
- Pause after the teacher has offered initial thinking
- Pause before paraphrasing
- Pause after a paraphrase

A Learning-focused Toolkit

## Applying Verbal Tools

Language and thinking are interactive processes. Each energizes the other. Each limits the other. The language choices supervisors make influence a teacher's readiness, confidence and ability to think. These strategic decisions shape expectations for the supervisory process and the working relationship. Thought-filled conversations combine non-verbal skills with the verbal tools of paraphrasing and inquiring.

This blend of tools affects the teacher's emotions and cognition. Learning-focused supervision is a developmental, growth-oriented model. As such, language that communicates the supervisor's belief in the teacher's motivation to continuously improve and ability to do so is critical. Word choice can stimulate both positive and negative responses. These subtle messages embedded in communication are called presuppositions.

### Expressing Belief in Capacity: The Positive Presupposition

All language expresses a supervisor's presuppositions about a teacher's professional abilities. For example, contrast the following:

*"Can you think of any ways to improve your classroom management?"*

Versus

*"Given the important connections between student learning and a well-managed classroom, what are some routines you are implementing?"*

Or

*"Do you see any ways that this student's work aligns with the writing rubric?"*

Versus

*"As you compare this student's writing to the rubric descriptors, what are some areas of alignment with the expectations for written expression that you're noticing?"*

While both inquiries are open-ended, the first examples question the capabilities of the teacher by communicating doubt in the teacher's awareness and ability to address the topic. The second examples express belief in the teacher's active and ongoing engagement with the topic. Our brains are wired to discern the embedded presupposition in each of these messages. Negative presuppositions inhibit thinking while positive presuppositions stimulate it. Skilled supervisors purposefully communicate positive presuppositions when working with their teachers.

### Shifting Language, Shifting Thought: Levels of Abstraction

Language is a system of agreed upon labels. For example, in English we understand that the 'thing' we sit around, set and dine upon is a table. We also understand that the word 'table' represents many types of this thing (coffee, dining, etc.) and that each of these labels also represent specific types; that is, a coffee table might be round, rectangular, high, low, of certain dimensions and so on. Therefore, knowing a language means we understand not just words, but those words in relation to the things (categories) and actions that they represent. When we hear or say the word table, we may be thinking of a particular item and we simultaneously understand the subsets that the word represents,

as well as the idea that the word, table, is itself a subset – of furniture, for example. Hayakawa (1964) describes these levels of language as a ladder of abstraction.

For skillful communicators, this concept suggests that all language resides at some level of abstraction. As described above, 'table' is an abstraction of all the types of tables we know. Abstractions, both mentally and linguistically, eliminate differences between things. This re-labeling is an indispensable aid to thoughtful and clear communication. When it is desirable to discuss broad themes and concepts, shifting up the ladder of abstraction allows for generalizations. For example, the paraphrase "so you're looking for dining room furniture" might move the conversation beyond a discussion about tables. By drilling down, that is exploring lower levels of abstraction, speaker and listener increase clarity about the topic of discussion. For example, the question, "When you say table, what are some of the qualities you are considering?" would likely produce a response that establishes specific parameters, dimensions, qualities, etc.

## Levels of Abstraction in Learning-focused Conversations

Defining is not the same as knowing. For example, a classroom teacher might be able to clearly define guided reading, but that doesn't mean he knows how to produce an effective guided reading lesson – or even recognize one being taught. If the supervisor's intention is to ground the conversation in specifics about the qualities of guided reading lessons, applying these qualities within the context of a specific classroom, or curriculum, then the exchange would be well-served by staying at lower levels of abstraction – at least initially. However, at some point, to effectively move beyond a single or highly specific context, for transfer and broader applications, higher levels of abstraction would be desirable and necessary.

Consider the following interaction. Note that in this conversation, with attention to levels of abstraction, both paraphrase and inquiry are applied to refine a general goal, e.g., do more with guided reading, into a measureable outcome. Both positive presuppositions and levels of abstraction are embedded in these verbal tools to increase thoughtfulness, by building confidence, offering choice, and defining vague areas.

T: *"One goal for me this year would be do to more with guided reading."*

S: *"So you're interested in adding to your present instructional approaches. Given what you know about your students, what are some things that led you to choosing guided reading?"*

T: *"Well, I know that guided reading is done with small groups, and that it is effective in producing more strategic readers. I already work with my kids in groups and they're used to that."*

S: *"One advantage, then, is that you can capitalize on your students' readiness to work in groups. What are some strategies you feel would be important at this point in your curriculum?"*

T: *"Well, they definitely need to strengthen their literal comprehension skills and their use of context clues, firm up sound/symbol relationships, especially consonant and vowel blends and for some of them, work on word structure, like syllabication and compound words."*

S: *"Given the array of skills you want to build, and your goal of using guided reading to do so, what kinds of assessments are you planning to determine their, and your, success?"*

**Ladder of Abstraction**

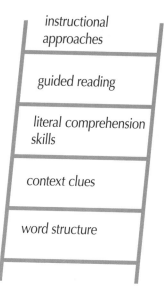

instructional approaches

guided reading

literal comprehension skills

context clues

word structure

A Learning-focused Toolkit

## Entering the Teacher's World: Using Paraphrase

A paraphrase is a response that reflects the meaning, or understood meaning, of a speaker by using different words to increase clarity. In learning-focused conversations, the purposeful use of paraphrase produces several positive results:

- It signals our full attention;
- It communicates that it is important to us to understand the teacher's thoughts, concerns, questions and ideas, thereby indicating the importance of the teacher, as well;
- It provides a launching point, connecting whatever follows, a question or suggestion for example, to the initial speaker's context or concern

Effective paraphrases align the speaker and responder, establishing understanding and communicating regard. With this foundation, we earn permission to inquire for details, press for elaboration or offer our own perspective or ideas. Without the paraphrase, inquiries can be perceived as interrogation, suggestions can be perceived as impositions.

Well-crafted paraphrases influence both relationship and cognition. The paraphrase reflects a speaker's thinking back to the speaker for further consideration, connecting the speaker and the listener in a flow of discourse. Combined with appropriate pauses, paraphrases trigger more thoughtful responses than questions alone.

## Three Types of Paraphrase, Three Intentions

Paraphrases label and reflect the speaker's content and often the speaker's emotions about the content. The ways in which this language is organized determines the type of paraphrase being offered. Three different paraphrase types, with three different intentions, widen the range of possible responses for learning-focused supervisors. Versatility in use of paraphrase gives a skillful supervisor a wide range of action from which to choose and a more effective repertoire for supporting growth.

The three types, or paraphrase categories, are Acknowledge and Clarify, Summarize and Organize and Shift Level of Abstraction. Each has a different, but related purpose. There is no formula for which paraphrase type to use at any given instance. The skilled supervisor attends fully to, both non-verbal and verbal cues, from the teacher and chooses accordingly.

### Acknowledge and Clarify

By restating the essence of someone's statements, acknowledge and clarify paraphrases provide an opportunity to identify and directly reflect content and emotions. The language in this paraphrase type is, essentially, on the same level of abstraction as the initial statement. By design, these paraphrases communicate our desire to understand, and our value for the person and what he or she is feeling and saying. Notice the intentional elimination of the personal pronoun 'I' in the paraphrase examples that follow.

For example, a teacher might say:

*"I don't know how I'll get all of this work done. I've got a final exam to correct, end-of-term grades and then the paperwork for closing the year!"*

To which a supervisor might respond:

*"So you're concerned about successfully completing the key end of year tasks in what feels like a very limited amount of time."*

## Summarize and Organize

Summarize and organize paraphrases offer themes and containers which shape the initiating statement or separate jumbled issues. This type of paraphrase is useful when there's been a great deal said in a long stream of language.

This type of paraphrase captures the key elements and offers some organization to which the speaker can react. It provides a 'shape' to the initiating statement. These organizing options include: containers or categories, compare/contrast, large themes, or a sequence or hierarchy.

For example, consider the following:

T: *"There are a number of key skills I know my students will need to be successful with the Common Core curriculum and I'm not sure if they are ready or if I have the instructional strategies for teaching them effectively."*

S: *"It seems there are several things on your mind, right now; identifying the explicit skills needed for success with the Common Core, getting your students ready to be successful and enhancing your own repertoire to ensure their success."* (Containers)

Or

T: *"I'm so confused. During language arts, my students work well in groups, participate in class and complete their assignments. In science, they are constantly off-task and I need to keep them doing individual work to keep control in the classroom."*

S: *"You're noticing significant differences between your students' performance in language arts and their performance in science."* (Compare/contrast)

Or

T: *"This teaching performance rubric clarifies expectations about classroom instruction and management as well as planning for effective teaching and ways to communicate and be professionally responsible in the school and community".*

S: *So, you're noting that high expectations for professional practice include both active classroom practice as well as performance outside the classroom."* (Themes)

Or

T: *"I'm thinking about setting up centers in my classroom and I also want to use some formative assessments as part of that and I'm not sure that my first graders are ready for the self-management needed to function in learning centers."*

S: *"Your sense is that, given your interest in establishing learning centers, you might first need to assess the behavioral skills needed for self-guided work, then determine which skills to teach and to whom, then establish centers that will be effective for the different levels of readiness."* (Sequence/hierarchy).

## A Scaffold for Crafting Paraphrases

Acknowledge and Clarify

- So, you're feeling _____
- You're noticing that _____
- In other words _____
- Hmm, you're suggesting that _____

Summarize and Organize

- So, there seem to be two key issues here _____ and _____
- On the one hand, there is _____ and on the other hand, there is _____
- For you then, several themes are emerging; _____
- It seems you're considering a sequence or hierarchy here; _____

Shifting Level of abstraction (Up or Down)

- So, a(n) _____ for you might be _____

| (Shifting up) | (Shifting down) |
| --- | --- |
| • category | • example |
| • value | • non-example |
| • belief | • choice |
| • assumption | • action |
| • goal | • option |
| • intention | |

## Shifting Level of Abstraction

The Shifting Level of Abstraction paraphrase reflects the speaker's language more globally or more specifically. These language shifts, in turn, influence the teacher's thinking. The intention of shifting up is to illuminate large ideas or categories, often leading the speaker to new discoveries, exploring potentially broad applications or determining possibilities for transfer. The shifting down paraphrase increases precision of thought and clarifies understanding for both parties.

When the conversation enters fairly abstract territory, or for individuals who think in highly global patterns, the shift down paraphrase is a way of grounding the thinking with specific examples and details. This, in turn, encourages the teacher to contribute additional descriptions and examples. For individuals who tend to think or speak in highly sequential and concrete patterns, shifting up opens a broader vista for exploration and provides a wider context for the topics at hand.

We move to higher levels of abstraction by naming the big ideas; including concepts, categories, goals and values. We move to lower levels of abstraction when concepts need grounding, offering specific examples or pertinent details.

For example, consider the following:

T: *"My kids have trouble getting started, and they're always asking for help."*

S: *"So, you want your students to be more self-reliant." (Shift Up)*

Or

S: *"For example, you're finding that your students' seem to be having trouble following directions." (Shift Down)*

A paraphrase that shifts to a higher level of abstraction is particularly effective in problem solving situations. Initially, more abstract language widens the potential solution set and encourages broader exploration of ideas and strategies for problem solving.

For example, consider this:

T: *"This math text is much too difficult for many of my students."*

S: *"So, you're looking for instructional materials that meet the needs of all of your students."*

This shift up paraphrase of math text to instructional materials opens the conversation to consider a wider range of solutions to this teacher's concern.

## Paraphrase and Problem Solving

In the hectic world of schools, time is a scarce commodity. Stopping to consider and frame issues productively often goes by the wayside in this frenzied environment. Sometimes everything seems equally urgent. As a result, during problem solving conversations, supervisors may find themselves interacting with teachers who are by degrees confused, overwhelmed, or reacting with strong feelings to an event or issue. At these times, teachers and supervisors are often their least flexible. Skillful and well-timed paraphrasing offers access to emotional resources, increasing readiness for addressing pressing issues.

**Four Do's of Paraphrase:**

- Avoid personal pronouns: "It seems to *me*...", "What *I* hear you saying..."

- Less is more: Keep the response shorter than the initiating statement

- Wait until the speaker is finished: Listen without interruption before paraphrasing

- Use tone to communicate intention: Invite confirmation or correction using an approachable voice

The human brain/body system does not make distinctions between feeling and thinking. As described earlier, biochemically we are one interconnected and interacting mix of molecules regulating hormonal responses and the production or suppression of the neurotransmitters that support higher level thinking. The molecules of emotion and the molecules of cognition respond in-the-moment to the influences of thoughtful interaction. At times like these, attentive supervisors strategically apply specific types of paraphrases to support the emotional and mental resourcefulness of their teachers. The goal paraphrase is especially effective in this regard. A goal paraphrase usually shifts the level of abstraction up, and works to illuminate potential outcomes. Once a goal becomes 'visible', emotional resourcefulness returns and the intellectual readiness for problem solving emerges.

## Well-Formed Goal Paraphrases

By attending fully to others and aligning physically, supervisors create the first level of psychological safety necessary for successful problem solving conversations. This skill couples with careful listening at multiple levels to the "story" being presented and to the "story-beneath-the story". Goal paraphrases are built on this listening beneath the story. Skillful supervisors are mindful that the listening blocks to understanding (personal, detail and certainty) inhibit the ability to produce this level of understanding. Goal paraphrases raise the level of abstraction of the initiating issue, making desired outcomes broadly visible and widening the solution set to increase problem-solving options. Consider the following:

> T: *"Some of my afternoon lab groups are unruly and are having difficulty focusing on the tasks and learning the material. They fool around for most of the period and then there's a mad rush to fill out the lab sheets at the end. All the attention is on completing the sheet and not on the processes of learning how to do science."*

> S: *So you want to feel confident that your students' energy is engaged in learning science process in your lab, not just doing the required worksheets.*

Head nods, postural shifts, changes in muscle tension and/or verbal responses are external cues that indicate internal shifts. By carefully monitoring these subtle signals, an alert supervisor recognizes when a proposed goal seems to fit for the teacher. Goal paraphrases offer a glimpse of a potential positive future. In this way, they provide an orientation that psychologically removes the other person from the muddle of the moment. When these possibilities align with the listener's context, related biochemical changes provide the necessary emotional and cognitive resources for problem solving.

Once the broad goal is established, for example, "You want to *feel respected* by your colleagues, the subsequent conversation works to clarify and define vague language. For example, the supervisor might ask, "What might be some *specific examples* of respect?" At this point, it is likely the teacher is ready to consider and identify potential actions towards achieving this goal.

## Verbal and Nonverbal Referencing

Gestural language and verbal language are linked systems. In many cases, such as problem solving conversations, the gestural vocabulary may carry information that amplifies and or extends the verbal portions. In some cases the body knows more than the mouth or knows it before we are able to construct language that understands and conveys the message.

### Tips for forming goal paraphrases

- When in doubt, offer fluffy goals.

  Raising the level of abstraction is especially useful when paraphrasing strong emotional messages.

- Listen for the central emotional component and flip it 180°.

  Respond to: "I'm totally overwhelmed by all the preparation I have to do, I have no life!"

  with "So, you want to feel some sense of *control and organization*."

A Learning-focused Toolkit

**Well-formed goal paraphrases:**

- Acknowledge the emotional components of the desired state – they are not limited to cognitive solutions.

    EX: "You want to be calm and feel prepared so you can have a successful presentation of your program at parents' night."

- Are stated in the positive – what the person wants, not what the person does not want.

    EX: "You'd like to have more efficient transitions between activities."

- Widen or broaden perspectives – offering a general 'destination' that can be refined as the conversation proceeds, not a 'journey' goal, naming the 'to-do's' of possible actions.

    EX: "So, you want to have more productive discussions in your literature class."

- Offer multiple possible solutions, not prescriptions. These are often stated as what the other person wants to 'feel', 'be', or 'have', not as what they are going to do.

    EX: "You want to feel a sense of accomplishment with these students."

    EX: "You want to be respected by your colleagues."

    EX: "You want to have a successful first marking period with your class."

- Summarize and organize conflicting or intertwined goals – issues often need to be separated in order to untangle elements that have jumbled together in the other person's mind.

    EX: "On the one hand, you'd like to have more personal time, and on the other, you want to feel well prepared for future lessons."

Attention to these nonverbal messages increases the effectiveness and efficiency of our communication. The subtle cues that are given and received maximize the clarity of the information and leads to greater productivity for both parties in the conversation. Aware supervisors attend to teacher's vocal patterns, such as rhythm, pitch and pace that indicate changes in thinking, or feeling; they consider intonation, emphasis and volume as cues to what might be important or of primary concern in the narrative. Similarly, lengthy pauses, sighs and repetition also provide meaningful signals.

Speakers place characters in space. It is useful to note how near, on which side and where the characters are in relation to each other. Speakers also place concepts in space. These are sometimes grouped and compared or contrasted nonverbally as the story details unfold. Time orientations are another form of gesture, for example, a hand from back to front or left to right indicating past, present and future. Gestural emphasis and patterns indicating a sequence or hierarchy of ideas or actions again give information about what might not be being said aloud, but what might matter to the speaker.

**Physical Referencing**

- Characters in space
- Concepts in space
- Sequence or hierarchy
- Time orientation

## Gestures with Paraphrase

Human nonverbal communication patterns are as rich and distinctive as spoken language. We have unique external cues to our internal thinking processes. While the patterns might be idiosyncratic, we can make some useful generalizations. For example, handedness plays a part in these patterns. Discerning hand dominance and observing marker cues is a useful communication tool. By noting where in space a speaker places story elements

## Mirror Neurons

Human beings have a rich repertoire of nonverbal expressions. The brain and the body are an integrated system. What is happening on the inside is reflected in sometimes subtle, and in other times overt ways by various parts of the body. In the early 1990's neuroscientists Vittorio Gallese and Giacomo Rizzolatti at the University of Parma in Italy discovered a new class of neurons in the brains of macaques, a species of monkey. They named their discovery mirror neurons. These cells are active in the brain when a monkey performs a physical movement such as grasping or pointing. The most important finding was that the same cells, or mirror neurons, are activated in the brains of other macaques that are observing these actions (Rizzolatti & Arbib, 1998).

Mirror neurons were soon discovered in human brains as well. Many researchers now think that these specialized brain cells provide the evolutionary and developmental link between gestural and verbal forms of communication (Motluk, 2001). In the human brain, major clusters of mirror neurons are located in the language processing and language production centers of the brain. These centers emerged 70,000 to 100,000 years ago making them relatively recent in our development as a species. They also appear slowly as human infants develop. Anyone who observes babies notices that gestures precede verbal skills as infants point at and clutch objects in their environment.

and characters, we can paraphrase both verbally and nonverbally by referencing these locations with our own gestures. Attentive supervisors watch for signs of cross-lateralization. The shift from left to right or right to left, indicates shifts across the corpus callosum which is the membrane that connects the brain's hemispheres. These shifts are external signs of brain integration and increasing efficacy towards problem solution.

Physical referencing is a subtle, but powerful skill that communicates understanding, increases psychological safety and mediates thinking. By paying attention to these elements as they are communicated, and continuing to develop increased acuity, an observant supervisor facilitates communication and accelerates learning.

| MARKER LANGUAGE | MARKER GESTURES |
|---|---|
| Verbal Stress | Physical Stress |
| • Volume | • Volume |
| • Emphasis | • Emphasis |
| Repetition | Repetition |
| Pace | Pace |
| Referencing | Referencing |

## Invitational Inquiry

Artful question construction is a powerful and learnable skill that combines with skillful pausing and paraphrasing to increase the learning potential of supervisory conversations. For many supervisors, thinking about inquiry in the context of learning-focused conversations requires a shift in intention. For skillful supervisors, inquiry is not about gathering information. The goal of inquiry is to produce thinking and to help the teacher integrate the self-talk of expertise. As a result, effective inquiries reflect this internal

dialogue and make it accessible to all practitioners. Compare the following questions in the context of a planning conversation:

*"In this interactive lesson, what size groups will you be forming?"*

Versus

*"In interactive lessons, what are some criteria you use to determine group size?"* (and then, perhaps, *"How are you applying those criteria to this lesson/class?"*)

Here is another example, in the context of a reflecting conversation:

*"These data indicate that you stayed in front of the class for 90% of the instructional time. What are some reasons you limited your movement?"*

Versus

*"These data indicate that you stayed in front of the class for 90% of the instructional time. What are some ways you monitor and choose where you position yourself in the classroom?"*

Note that in both first examples the supervisor is, essentially, gathering information. In the second questions, the supervisor is inquiring into the teacher's thinking and, ideally, is offering questions that the teacher will continue to ask herself when planning or reflecting upon instruction. In addition, these thought-provoking questions are intended for potential generalization. For example, "In this interactive lesson . . . " as compared with "In interactive lessons . . .". This concept, that inquiry is first and foremost about increasing a teacher's capacity for self-directed learning, is fundamental to keeping supervision learning-focused.

## Designing Questions to Promote Thinking

Skillful supervisors are purposeful in their use of questions. A supervisor's linguistic repertoire includes the capacity to frame language that broadens thinking, as well as language that focuses thinking. These questions communicate a spirit of curiosity and a desire to explore information and ideas. Each category of questions influences thinking. Questions that broaden thinking invite responses that offer multiple and expanded ideas and thoughts. These questions elicit concepts, categories, and generalizations. Questions that focus thinking still harvest multiple responses, but probe for increased specificity of information. These questions elicit examples, criteria, and details that support precision in verbal responses and greater precision in thinking. Both types of questions are an important part of the learning-focused supervisor's repertoire. Both types of questions contain verbal and nonverbal elements designed to invite thinking.

**Invitational Inquiry**

Broadening thinking

Focusing thinking

## Creating the Conditions for Thinking

To respond thoughtfully to rich and purposeful inquiry requires emotional readiness on the teacher's part. The full array of verbal and non-verbal skills is at play here. Paraphrase is one component that creates the emotional readiness to respond to inquiries that require thoughtful responses. It works in concert with the non-verbal skills described above and fits within a pattern that paces the conversation for thinking, interspersing functional pauses before and after paraphrasing and inquiring. Inquiry delves into what is not yet known, or readily available. Thus it is necessary for the teacher to be willing to deal with the discomfort of 'not knowing' and be open to discovery during the supervisory exchange.

**Pattern of discourse**

*so, new into.*

listen/
    pause/
        paraphrase/
           pause/
               inquire

Questions that extend and illuminate thinking invite a wide range of potential responses. Inviting thinking begins with eliciting these verbal responses. Language and thinking once surfaced can always be honed and refined. But without it emerging, there is little with which to work. Well-crafted inquiries integrate three essential elements; an invitation to engage, a cognitive process to focus thinking and a topic, or something to think about. Given personal style and context, these elements can be combined in a variety of ways and do not always appear in the same order. The interplay of these elements creates the emotional and cognitive context for the engagement.

## Template for Inquiry

Effective inquires signal the supervisor's desire to explore ideas and communicate a belief in the teacher's capacity, readiness and willingness to think out loud. A blend of tonal and linguistic components shapes well-crafted inquiries. This section describes the three interchangeable elements: an invitation to engage, a cognitive focus and a topic.

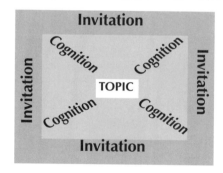

### The Invitation

The invitation to think functions as a total package that wraps around our communication. This invitation begins with clear signals that our full presence is available for this conversation and that we intend no harm. This invitation has two primary layers: tonal and syntactical. Listeners automatically assess the tone of the words they are hearing for any signs of threat. This rapidly firing safety assessment influences both what we hear and how we process the incoming information. Interpreting the syntactical structure of the message is the next filtering system in the human brain. We analyze linguistic messages for both the type of responses that are being requested and for the degree of psychological safety that ultimately determines how forthcoming we are with our answers.

### The Tonal Layer

*Approachable Voice.* An approachable voice for framing language in a nonthreatening manner creates the tonal layer in the invitation. We learned this pattern from Michael Grinder, a classroom management expert and specialist in nonverbal patterns of communication (Grinder, 1997). An approachable voice is well modulated and rhythmic, with the tone rising at the end of the question. This signals a sense of openness and exploration that the teacher interprets as a request for participation. This intonation contrasts with the credible voice, which is more evenly modulated with a flatter tone and drops at the end of a statement. This voice pattern indicates that the speaker is sharing information and expertise. Voice choice signals the stance within which we are operating. The more approachable voice indicates a coaching stance; the more credible voice indicates a calibrating or consulting stance.

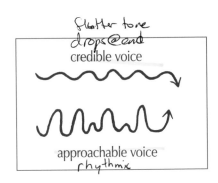

### The Syntactical Layer

The syntactical choices that we make influence the way teachers respond to our questions. These subtle elements encourage or inhibit thinking and the quality of the teacher's answers.

Three key syntactical choices make it emotionally easier for the teacher to think and increase the options for thinking: plural forms, exploratory language and non-dichotomous forms.

*Plural Forms.* Plural forms indicate that there are multiple possible responses; for example, *goals* instead of *goal, concerns* rather than *concern*. Combined with an approachable intonation, this pattern suggests that all responses at this point have merit, and frees the teacher from having to evaluate and sort.

*Exploratory Language.* Exploratory language has a tentative quality. Examples include words like *some, might, seems, possible* and *hunches*. These terms, like the use of plurals, widen the potential range of response and reduce the need for surety. Words like *could* and *why* tend to decrease the confidence of teachers who may interpret these words as questioning their capabilities for thought or indicate the need to justify their choices and actions. In addition the word *could,* as in the question, "Given this issue, what *could* you do about it?" may interrupt thought processes by seeming to require a commitment to ideas or actions that the teacher is not yet ready to make. The use of why in an inquiry requires the responder to explain or defend their thinking. Further, the connotation is that you need to explain or defend your response to me, the supervisor.

Consider these examples:

*"What is the best way you could meet these students' learning needs?"*

Versus

*"What seem to be some ways you might address these students' learning needs?"* Or

*"Why did you use that example at that point in the lesson?"*

Versus

*"What were some reasons for offering that example at that point in the lesson?"*

*Non-dichotomous Forms.* The third syntactical component of the invitation is the use of non-dichotomous question forms. Dichotomous questions are those that can be answered yes or no, true or false, is or is not. In contrast, questions that invite thinking are framed with open-ended, non-dichotomous forms. For example, instead of asking *"Did you notice any unusual behaviors?"*, ask *"What are some of the behaviors you noticed?"* When we use dichotomous forms, we actually communicate doubt in capacity. For example, *"Have you thought about these data as you plan for next week's instruction?"*, might suggest the supervisor's doubt that the data have been incorporated or are considered in planning on a consistent basis. Contrast that form with, *"What are some ways that these data are influencing your planning for next week's instruction?"*.

By eliminating dichotomous stems such as *"Can you," "Did you," "Will you,"* or *"Have you"* we invite thinking and communicate positive presuppositions about the teacher's capacity and willingness to think (see pg. 32).

## Providing Cognitive Focus

Learning-focused supervisors craft inquiries that are purposefully driven by clear cognitive intentions. The effectiveness and efficiency of planning, problem solving and reflecting is amplified by targeting specific thinking processes. For example, teachers develop expertise in planning by identifying, predicting and sequencing. Similarly, teachers make sense of experience by inferring, comparing and analyzing cause and effect. Productive reflection derives from generalizing, hypothesizing, applying and synthesizing. Questions that invite and focus thinking build professional capacity and self-directed learning. Embedded within each phase of the Conversation Templates described in Chapter Three are verbs that promote specific cognitive processes.

## Directing the Inquiry: The Topic

Question topics range in degree of directness. The choice of language for the topic of a question influences this key variable. Potential topics can range from higher to lower levels of abstraction. Inquiries with topics at higher levels of abstraction stimulate a broader range of responses. Inquiries with topics at lower levels of abstraction narrow the focus of the responses. For example, a question topic might be classroom management. Staying at a higher level of abstraction, the supervisor might ask, *"What are some ways you monitor classroom management procedures?"* The response categories might include instructional grouping, managing materials, or record keeping. Or lowering the level of abstraction, the topic could be student transitions, *"What are some ways you monitor student transitions?"*

### Syntactical Substitutions

The ---- Some

Is -- Seems

Could – Might

Why ----What

### Stems to Convey Positive Presuppositions

Given your knowledge of …

Based on your experience with…

Reflecting on . . .

As you consider…

*Intentional inciting questions*

In this example, the responses migh be directed towards maximizing instructional time, student clarity about what to do and where to move, or giving clear directions about expectations. Higher levels of abstraction include the names of teaching domains, in this case Classroom Environment. Lower levels of abstraction include indicators, critical attributes or specific examples.

Focusing the topic increases the time efficiency of the conversation by allowing the supervisor to go directly to critical areas, while still inviting teacher thinking about the topic. Further, a more directed question feels safer for the teacher, because there is less ambiguity about potential appropriate responses.

## Inquiry to Focus Thinking

There is much more information in our environment then ever appears in our language. Our brains filter incoming information, searching for recognizable patterns. From these, we form meanings about the world, and mental models that shape and guide thinking and ultimately behavior. Human language reflects these thinking habits, resulting in surface vagueness that often masks or obscures the rich details that lie beneath.

For example, in describing her class, a teacher might simply say, *"my students are really coming along in learning to cooperate."* Beneath this surface statement is her delight that they are following routines, working well in groups, being responsible for classroom materials and are increasingly self-reliant. However, without inquiring for these details, that information is not available for exploration.

Inquiring for more specificity in a learning-focused conversation is important for several reasons. First, to be sure that there is a shared understanding of what seems very clear to one party, but might be interpreted differently by the other. For example, the teacher implicitly defines 'coming along in learning to cooperate' as the variety of details offered above. The supervisor might suppose she means that they are cooperating with her, not necessarily with one another and assume that they are listening to directions, handing in assignments and adhering to classroom rules. Without inquiring, a very different take on the exchange, and understanding of the teacher's perspective, might result. These inquiries also serve to illuminate examples, details and actions that define goals, increase clarity of thinking for the teacher and may be critical to agreed upon professional development plans.

In addition, by focusing on and clarifying specifics, an attentive supervisor can help shift a situation from one that might feel overwhelming to one that is more manageable emotionally, physically and intellectually. Like many supervisory skills, inquiring for specificity is based on listening. In this case, the skill set is listening for vague language and then deciding which terms, if clarified, would support the most productive shifts in thinking. For a clearer idea of what might produce vague language, it is important to understand the internal processes that produce it.

### Deletions, Generalizations and Distortions

Our brains create and are created by models of reality built from our experiences in the world and from our interpretations of those experiences. As a result, three internal processes shape what appears in surface language: deletions, distortions and generalizations (Bandler & Grinder, 1971). We delete and distort incoming and outgoing

data to fit deeply embedded mental templates. We generalize as a kind of short cut to making sense of our experience. These processes are not conscious on the speaker's part.

Vague language occurs when we delete or generalize. It is useful to understand these two categories as they become important listening lenses for the attuned supervisor who selects a focus for clarification, paraphrases the essential ideas, then inquires to increase specificity within target areas. In many cases, more than one category of vagueness occurs in the same statement. In all cases, the skillful supervisor applies the pattern of pause, paraphrase and then inquire.

## Deletions

We delete when we overlook or omit information, either incoming or outgoing. In spoken, and written language these deletions appear as vague nouns, vague pronouns and vague verbs. For example, the speaker omits the qualities of the verb *appreciate,* or the number of *parents* who help their students do homework, or the percentage of units that are effective in the *curriculum.* Let's take another look at the example above:

*"My students are really coming along in learning to cooperate."*

There are several deletions here, including the qualities of cooperation, with whom the students are cooperating, which students specifically are improving and in what ways. By inquiring into any of these deletions, an attentive supervisor increases clarity in the conversation and precision in thinking for the teacher. For example, the supervisor might ask, *"What are some examples of cooperative student behaviors that you are seeing at this point in the school year?"*

For supervisors, careful listening helps to inform the construction of questions that will support precision. On a regular basis, one hears conversational exchanges that include: *'my students', 'the class', 'my fourth period', 'classroom management', 'student behavior', 'technology', 'the parents', 'the administration', 'central office'* and a host of other unspecified nouns. For many teachers, someone named *'they'* causes most of the problems in their class or school. *'We', 'us',* and *'them'* are other possible sources of concern and/or joy.

In a learning-focused conversation, if we hear a teacher say, *"my students don't understand fractions,"* it is important to find out how many students are confused about fractions and what elements of fraction learning are most problematic to them. Without these essential details, we can't know where to target our energy and attention within the problem solving process. Narrowing the field of focus in this case might identify subsets of students with distinct learning needs that can be addressed systematically by the teacher for working with the students.

Planning, problem solving and reflecting require specificity for focused action and personal learning. The term *'understand'* in the example above is a prime example. Once we have determined who has the problem, we need to clarify the goal of understanding. What does this teacher mean by 'understanding'; and how will students display their own 'understanding'? With some teachers, these specifications may lead to unpacking their own understanding of fractions as well.

Teacher goal setting is a particularly important area for clarifying action. Words like; *'plan', 'improve', 'design', 'modify', 'enhance'* and *'prepare'* are all examples of unspecified verbs that have little meaning without clarification and details.

### Deletions

**Vague nouns**
my students, the class, my fourth period, central office

**Vague pronouns**
they, we, them, us

**Vague verbs**
understand, appreciate, control, prepare, design

*Important to narrow the field & get more focused.*

*Additional Deletions*

Another common linguistic deletion when the speaker omits the criteria that is the basis of a comparison or reference point for a comparison. For example, when a teacher says, *"Today's lesson was much better,"* two queries might be productive; *"In what ways was it better?"* and/or *"What was it better than?"* Until we discover the speaker's criteria for *'better'*, we don't know how to proceed with the conversation. Is this *'better'* a success to build on or are poorly understood factors at work here that leave this *'better'* a mystery? Other vague comparators are words like *'best'*, *'larger'*, *'slower,'* *'more'*, *'less'* and *'least'*.

Learning-focused supervisors support teachers by helping them to specify their criteria and standards for comparison. This action supports rigor in planning and problem solving, which leads to targeted action and measurable signs of success. When a teacher says *"I want students to get better results on my next quiz,"* a supervisor might respond by probing for the qualities that would define better results. For example, does the teacher mean a higher class average or some other improvements in student responses?

We also often need to surface the missing reference, or lost comparator. For example, was this lesson better than the best lesson the teacher has taught to date—or better than the worst? Our continued conversation would be quite different, depending upon the response.

## Generalizations

Generalizations are the brain's way of efficiently cataloging experience by placing a value on it for later reference. Generalizations are useful because we rely on these judgments when making additional choices. For example, if my experience with liquid detergent, perhaps even a specific brand, versus powder has been positive, I will look for liquid detergent when shopping and not need to stop and analyze my choices each time. However, we get into trouble when we generalize from too little experience or when we don't periodically stop to consciously review our present generalizations. For example, a teacher attends a workshop that does not meet his needs and forms the impression, or creates a generalization that all professional development is ineffective based on this one experience, and avoids seeking any additional learning opportunities..

We all have a set of rules that guide our ways of perceiving and operating in the world. We are not always conscious of these internal codes but they appear in our language when we say things like, *"I have to,"* *"I must,"* *"I can't,"* and *"I should have"* or *"I shouldn't have."* Many times these rules are generalized from little or no longer relevant experience. For example, if a teacher says, *"I can't let my students work in teams because they won't get any work done,"* the supervisor needs to carefully paraphrase and explore the reasons beneath the statement. For example she might say, *"You have some concerns about group work. What are some of your assumptions about the skills and attitudes your students might need to get the most out of learning together?"* Intonation matters greatly here. The supervisor's voice must be carefully modulated: nonthreatening intonation is key to creating a safe environment for exploring the internal rules governing the situation.

Another common form of generalization is what linguists label as universal quantifiers. Words and phrases like *'everyone'*, *'all'*, *'no one'*, *'never'* and *'always'* are often spoken as if the statement possesses a universal truth of which *'everyone'* is aware. By clarifying these terms, a supervisor helps the teacher ground the conversation with measurable details and supportable data. When the teacher says, *"No one in my class completes their*

**Additional Deletions**

**Comparators:**

better, slower, more, least

**Generalizations**

**Rules:** "I have to";
"we should"

**Universal Quantifiers:**
"you always. . ."
"I never. . .",
"everyone thinks . . ."

*assignment,"* the supervisor might respond with a paraphrase and then inquire: *"Your students are having some trouble getting their work done. Which of your students seem to be having the most difficulty finishing their work?"*

The teacher reporting that her students are *'coming along'* may be a generalization. That would depend on how frequently and consistently she is seeing the behaviors she describes as cooperative. It is possible she is exhilarated by the success of one lesson. It is also possible that she has been monitoring performance in the critical attributes of cooperation for several weeks. Again, a thoughtful and well-framed inquiry clarifies and illuminates. A supervisor might ask, *"As you think about the increase in cooperative behaviors, what percentage of the time would you say your students' display these skills?"* Or, *"what percentage of your students have demonstrated marked improvement in their cooperative skills?"*

The Learning-Focused Toolkit is a vital resource for skillful communication with teachers as supervisors help them to plan, problem-solve and reflect on practice. While the tools of pausing, paraphrasing and inquiring operate in concert with one another they are easier to learn in isolation so that each can be used automatically in a variety of settings. Purposeful practice of the each tool individually leads to skills integration for fluent application within Planning and Reflecting Conversations and fluid navigation of the Continuum of Learning-focused Interaction.

# 5. Learning-focused Supervision: Developing Expertise

No one is born knowing how to teach. Classroom instruction is one of the most complex intellectual and emotional tasks that any professional undertakes in our society; and the journey towards expertise is a lifetime's work.

Successful journeys are guided by skilled counsel. For the learning to be increasingly purposeful, supervisors need frameworks and language for describing the complexity of teaching. This complexity falls into two main areas: what professional teachers think about and pay attention to in their classrooms; and how they think about it before, during and after instruction. This knowledge base organizes the expert teacher's planning, problem solving and decision-making. Mental access to these resources supports effective teaching practice that is goal-driven and targeted to the needs of individual students. These capabilities, brought to conscious attention, then guide the supervisor's own interactions with teachers.

## Developing a Vision of Learning

Learning to teach means continually managing the disequilibrium that new questions and newly recognized quandaries produce. Given the limits of attention and the limits of craft knowledge, some teachers do not know what they do not know.

Supervision, therefore, means a continual balance of supporting current learning needs for teachers, with providing appropriate challenges for growth at opportune moments. It also means acknowledging the sense of loss and lowered confidence that often accompanies new awareness of knowledge and skill gaps. These are territories of constructive mismatch that require emotional sensitivity and scrupulous attention to the teacher's current emotional state and developmental level. The information on teaching expertise outlined in this section is intended to focus the supervisor's attention and frame this learning agenda. School-based curriculum initiatives, such as the Common Core, intersect with this repertoire to promote collegiality and learning communities in the school.

According to Jean Piaget, learning is a process of disturbing current constructs with new experiences and exposure to novel ideas. These discoveries then need to be assimilated and/or accommodated to form new conceptual understandings. Skillful supervisors know when and how to gently disturb a teacher's current state of development as they escort them on their journey to more expert teaching.

## Defining and Developing Expertise

Developing expertise in any field involves the acquisition, storage and contextually appropriate application of knowledge and skills. A defining characteristic of experts is the ways in which this knowledge base is mentally structured and internally cross-referenced for productive application in both predictable and novel situations. As teachers become increasingly skillful they develop both rich conceptual bases and more extensive case knowledge. Case knowledge is the treasure trove of practical experiences that experts draw upon to solve routine problems. These are the tricks-of-the trade that make professional practice time and energy efficient.

Expert teachers are able to operate both in the moment and over time with clear outcomes in mind; skillfully managing students, content, equipment, materials, the clock and the calendar. They also apply greater complexity and sophistication in analyzing and understanding instructional problems. For example, while managing student learning, master teachers focus first on defining and representing the dilemmas they encounter in their classrooms. In contrast, beginning teachers go directly to developing solutions without first framing the problem (Swanson, O'Connor, and, Cooney, 1990). This difference in the approach to problem solving is one reason for the importance of a strategy like the Think-Aloud. By thinking aloud about a problem when taking the consulting stance, a supervisor models how an 'expert' contemplates a situation, thereby widening the conceptual, emotional and moral frame for the teacher.

Experience and expertise are not the same thing. Experts in all fields develop sophisticated sets of guiding principles, templates and tools to apply to the problems they encounter. The hallmarks of expertise are knowing which principles and tools to apply to a given situation, the limits of these resources and when current templates and tools need to be modified or adapted to better match present requirements.

As we think about the role of supervisors as growth agents in helping to develop teachers' skills, it is useful to consider the nature of learning and the structure of expertise. The following five principles emerge from the literature on expert problem solving and expert teaching.

## 1.   Expertise develops from frameworks of experience, culture and context.

Expert thinkers are aware of the influence of their previous experiences on the ways in which they perceive and approach their practice. Teacher's behaviors and patterns of thinking are guided by their beliefs, values and principles (Clark & Peterson, 1998). Growth oriented supervisors help teachers surface and articulate the background experiences and the frameworks they hold. This conceptual and cultural knowledge can then be compared to that of students, parents and colleagues as a point of reference for planning, problem solving and reflecting.

During learning-focused conversations, a skillful supervisor discovers what and how teachers think in relation to a specific situation. The supervisor can then illuminate potential misconceptions, biases or gaps in thinking and offer alternative perspectives and ways of thinking about the issue or situation.

Ways of understanding are idiosyncratic. Teachers as learners construct meaning based on their beliefs, understandings and prior experiences. Mindful supervisors respect the interests and passions of their teachers – what they know, where they've been, what inspires them, what they are able to do and what they'd like to be able to do. The supervisor can then support the teacher in bridging prior experiences and new ideas.

## 2.   Expert thinking is organized by big ideas and core concepts.

How knowledge is organized matters. Experts develop mental clusters of interrelated information (Bransford, et al, 1999). Each cluster has distinctive elements and features that are mentally flagged for ease of retrieval. Experts have more available information units than non-experts. Experts organize these mental clusters for accessibility so they retrieve and apply knowledge and skills to different problem solving situations (Chi, et. al, 1981).

Expert teachers have organizers with conceptual labels stored in their long-term memories. These interrelated categories are efficiently accessed to make sense of practice, to support planning and to guide classroom decisions and actions. These categories help teachers plan curricula, differentiate instruction and analyze student work.

Experts know their way around the landscape. They are familiar with significant features and are able to locate and use available resources (Greeno, 1991). Knowing where one is in a landscape requires a network of connections that link the present location to the larger space. Within the classroom landscape, expert teachers are able to articulate their perspectives and the ways of seeing and perceiving that they draw upon to make decisions and solve problems (Bransford, 1986).

Skilled supervisors use learning-focused conversations to help teachers connect broader principles of practice to specific solutions and strategies. By moving beyond the isolated parts, these supervisors orient teachers to a larger view of professional practice. These connections are often accomplished with by using a pattern of explaining the "What", "Why", and "How" of an approach or strategy when taking a consulting stance, or offering a principle of practice to provide a wide view.

Skilled supervisors inquire into their teachers' thinking to determine which connections are being made, where gaps exist and to note the width and depth of the frame for holding a given situation or problem. They also ask teachers to describe the reasons for the choices they are making related to instruction, curriculum and student and parent interactions. When any gaps surface, the needed information or perspectives can be offered.

## 3.  Experts frame and reframe problems before seeking solutions.

The way in which a problem is framed either expands or limits the possible solutions that might be generated and applied to it. The literature on expert problem solving refers to this phenomena as problem setting (Grimett, 1988, Schon, 1983). Real world problems do not come with givens. They arise within situations that are troubling and uncertain. The ways in which a problem is set frames the boundaries of our attention and supplies any sense of coherence that identifies what is wrong within the situation. These problem frames point out the potential direction of any changes we might make. During problem setting we notice the things to which we might pay attention and develop the context within which we will attend to them (Schon, 1983).

Experts have greater acuity for problem elements and conscious lenses for examining issues from a variety of perspectives. Experts often frame and reframe problems before pursuing solutions.

Skilled supervisors help teachers define professional problems. They purposely and overtly offer problem frames before offering solutions, strategies and approaches. These, "here's how I think about that" exchanges from a consulting stance are opportunities to introduce ideas, applications and principles of practice.

These supervisors invite their teachers to join them in problem framing conversations. As the relationship unfolds, and in developmentally appropriate ways, they support teachers in developing these patterns of thinking. This approach is especially important if patterns of problem types emerge within the teacher's classroom practice and/or within learning-focused conversations.

## 4.   Expertise results from internal and external mediation.

The self-talk of experts differs greatly from that of less effective practitioners. Expert teachers develop and internalize patterns and behaviors that free their attention for the more interactive and dynamic needs of classroom practice. Expert teachers automatize routines for management tasks like taking attendance and focusing students' attention (Leinhardt and Greeno, 1986, Berliner, 1987). They have mental scripts (Shavelson, 1986, and Berliner, 1987) for tasks like monitoring student understanding, giving directions and varying call and response patterns. These micro-maps and moves free attention for more subtle student-centered interactions and responses. Less effective teachers tend to notice and respond to discreet instances and events in isolation. Developing instructional routines and automatizing repertoire are building blocks to expert practice.

Skilled supervisors make their internal self-talk overt and explicit when talking with teachers. They share the concepts they draw upon, the connections they are making and the ways in which they perceive and frame issues. Such supervisors offer broad terms rather than singular examples as they talk about such things as goals, outcomes, routines, cues and signals. In this way, they supply categories for holding and connecting information that can be accessed by the teacher at a later time.

Skilled supervisors mediate thinking and prompt metacognition, inviting the teacher to notice and reflect upon his or her own patterns of thinking and problem solving. For example, during planning conversations, the supervisor supports thinking about goal identification and indicators of success, designing coherent instruction and using assessment data to make decisions. With sufficient supported practice, the teacher internalizes and applies this type of thinking independently. The challenge for supervisors is to find the appropriate balance between promoting a teacher's rapid development of needed skills and routines and promoting the deeper understandings about principles of practice to support more independent growth.

## 5.   Experts recognize the limitations of their own knowledge base and seek resources and strategies to increase their proficiency.

Disequilibrium and the uncertainty of not knowing are milestones on the pathway to any new learning. Knowing what one does not know is as important a learning resource as knowing what one does know (Lipton and Wellman, 2000). The ability to recognize the limitations in one's current knowledge base and developing the confidence to seek new strategies and information are essential to learning, and to teaching. The ability to monitor one's present level of understanding and decide when more information or resources are necessary is an important characteristic of expertise.

Skillful supervisors offer appropriate formative assessment during learning-focused conversations. This focused feedback increases the teacher's capacity for on-going self-assessment. Clear, nonjudgmental feedback offers evidence of success as well as the information to clarify ideas and identify misconceptions.

These supervisors help teachers move beyond simply learning to perform specific procedures or apply specific strategies in isolated contexts. Through coaching, collaborating and consulting they promote transfer of ideas between content areas, topics and situations. The most effective transfer comes from the balance between specific examples, generalizable principles and clear criteria for measuring success. This learning-

focused feedback, builds the capacity for determining increasingly effective actions leading to continuous improvements in practice.

## Acquiring Craft Knowledge

Day-to-day classroom work draws upon a reservoir of craft knowledge for planning instruction, solving problems and analyzing effectiveness. This sophisticated knowledge base is acquired through the years as teachers master the various tasks required by their work. In the 1980's, Donald Schon described this wisdom in his seminal work on reflective practice (Schon 1983; 1987). Schon suggests that experienced professionals rely very little on theoretical or academic knowledge to solve practical problems. They rely instead on an extensive body of context specific craft knowledge that allows them to relate past experiences to current situations. Thus, the primary source for learning for experienced teachers is, in fact, reflection on their own practice.

To access this learning, and to apply the wisdom of practice to new and novel contexts, teachers need to be able to unpack the purposes and processes of automated routines, and to bring them to their own conscious awareness. The opportunity to explore instructional decisions, and to analyze their effectiveness is one of the gifts of the supervisor/teacher relationship. Articulating one's own craft knowledge increases its usefulness and extends the craftsmanship and capacity of the user.

Craft knowledge and expertise in teaching take time to acquire. This growth occurs in predictable stages. David Berliner suggests the following five developmental stages (Calderhead, 1996).

---

### Novice to Expert Stages of Teacher Development

1. Novice: Seeking rules and recipes to guide actions.

2. Advanced Beginner: Seeking contextual and strategic knowledge and beginning to understand when the rules are appropriate and when they might be broken.

3. Competent: Making conscious choices about what to do and how to monitor and modify actions to meet goals.

4. Proficient: Operating intuitively with know-how, viewing actions holistically within both short and long term goals.

5. Expert: Integrating the teacher and the task, operating fluently with automaticity and few surprises, in control of the situation.

---

## Novice Teachers

Novice teachers seek the comfort of rules and procedures for guidance. With little repertoire to draw from, they attempt to duplicate the structured lessons in the teacher's manual. This might mean preparing and implementing a guided reading lesson for a specific story in the precise sequence described in the district's reading text. Initially, there is little variation from the scripted text and scant attention to individual student responses. The novice presents the lesson as written in the manual, following her advanced preparation.

### Advanced Beginner Teachers

Advanced Beginners start to stretch the pattern a bit. They are at the early stages of developing richer knowledge about basic classroom operations, their students and teaching specific subjects. For example, they still might use the reading series as a foundation for lessons, but with a bit more comfort and confidence in basic routines, they add strategies like experiential language charts to expand the lesson structure. They also might modify the sequence that the publisher suggests, incorporating tips from colleagues as they develop personal preferences in both stories and techniques.

### Competent Teachers

Competent teachers are goal oriented across a spectrum of instructional concerns. They have the ability to change course during lessons to better meet the immediate needs of learners. During the planning and teaching of a reading lesson, for example, they consider the needs of specific learners and tailor the lesson to help each student develop literacy skills. Assessment of student progress is ongoing and shapes each day's lesson design. The teacher's manual no longer controls instructional practice.

### Proficient Teachers

Proficient teachers operate at multiple levels simultaneously. They have goals for the class, goals for each student and goals for themselves. They skillfully organize instruction that has both short-term and long-term coherence. Reading lessons, which extend throughout the day and across the curriculum, are not limited to a special period. Students are flexibly grouped and regrouped as skills develop. There is increased attention and greater sophistication in applying informal and formal assessments. These are used to organize differentiated lessons and to form specialized groups.

### Expert Teachers

Expert teachers expand personal and professional proficiency in all areas of their teaching. There is an organic flow to the day that extends to the ways students self-manage many classroom routines. Teachers at this stage anticipate potential management and learning bottlenecks and intervene before problems emerge. They are able to fluidly apply a vast technical repertoire of knowledge and skills about learning and learners. While seeing children as unique individuals, their personal catalog of learner types helps them to assemble targeted materials and lessons that smooth learning pathways. This confidence and comfort allows them to establish routines that promote independence and students' sense of personal responsibility for learning outcomes. Individual and small group conferences enhance students' abilities to self-assess and make appropriate learning choices.

## Transitioning From Novice to Expert

According to Berliner, the novice stage occupies the first year of teaching. Most teachers reach the competent stage after three or four years, with only a modest proportion moving to the proficient stage and fewer still attaining expert status. The growth from novice to more expert teaching requires more than simple experience. It is also a highly personal voyage through the seas of adult development. Having a skilled navigator along to plot

**Using Reading Instruction to Illustrate Stages of Teacher Development**

Novice: Seeks rules and recipes to guide actions.

A guided reading lesson is prepared and implemented in the exact method and sequence described in the teacher's manual. There is little variation from the scripted text and scant attention to the student responses.

Advanced Beginner: Seeks contextual and strategic knowledge; beginning to stretch beyond the prescribed lesson.

The reading series is still the foundation for the lesson, but increased confidence and developing personal style allow for enhancements. For example, an experiential language chart might be used to expand the lesson structure. Sequence of instruction might be modified to better meet student needs, or to adjust to schedule constraints.

Competent: Makes intentional choices about what to do and how to monitor and modify actions to meet goals.

Knowledge of specific learners is applied to the reading lesson planning. In planning and implementation, the lesson is tailored to help each student develop literacy skills, as needed. Reading groups are flexible and multiple methods are drawn upon to support learning.

Proficient: Operates intuitively with know-how, viewing actions holistically across both short and long term goals.

Reading lessons extend throughout the day and are part of content area instruction. There is increased attention and greater sophistication in applying formal and informal reading assessment to monitor student progress and target student needs. Special interest reading and writing centers are central to the learning, providing for differentiated skill development and in-depth exploration of a variety of topics.

Expert: Integrates the teacher and the task, in control of the classroom, operating fluently with few surprises.

Reading routines promote students' independence and personal responsibility for meeting learning goals. Individual and small group conferencing, self-directed projects and self-assessment inventories enhance students' abilities to analyze their own progress, set new goals and pursue increasingly sophisticated learning outcomes.

Source: Lipton, L. & Wellman, B. (2003). Making Mentoring Work: An ASCD Action Tool Alexandria, VA: ASCD

---

the course and find safe harbors increases the safety of the journey and allows one to enjoy the adventure. Skilled supervisors come equipped with a chart, a compass, and knowledge of the route ahead.

## Metacognition as an Organizer for Professional Practice

Experts think differently about their practice than do less effective practitioners. They also think about their thinking differently. Metacognition refers to two aspects of complex thinking processes. One is awareness of one's thinking processes while they are occurring. The other is the self-regulation of these processes.

Expert teachers exercise metacognitive skills in a variety of ways, monitoring decisions, choices and the impact of actions. This is the inner voice of expertise. As they access this resource, master teachers continually sort through their internalized knowledge-bases about the structure of the discipline they are currently teaching, their instructional repertoire, knowledge of the individual students with whom they are working and knowledge about their own goals, values and beliefs. We describe these knowledge-bases in more detail later in this section. As they sort this treasure-trove of options, master teachers mentally articulate and apply clear criteria for their selections.

It is the kinds and qualities of their filters that most separates experts from novices. Expert teachers are able to pursue multiple goals for a wider variety of students during the flow of the lesson than are novices. They always have big picture outcomes for thinking and social skills and continually reinforce them. They manage relationships with the whole class at the same time that they intervene with and support individual learners. Experts design specific lessons that fit within a bigger curriculum plan that is operating all the time. Novice teachers tend to be more immediate, intent on managing the flow of a specific lesson plan or controlling student behavior.

Self-regulation of thinking processes is the essence of intention-driven action in the classroom. This vital feedback loop helps alert teachers calibrate their choices and behaviors with their intentions, encouraging in-flight reflection and self-monitoring. This attention might mean monitoring the pace of one's speech and use of pauses to elicit student thinking. It also might mean controlling emotions when responding to a difficult student. In essence, it is the thermostat of self-control that regulates attention, task-focus, impulsiveness, humor and a host of emotional, mental and physical responses.

---

### An Expert Teacher's Metacognition

A skilled chemistry teacher notices something is not right in her classroom. The noise level and level of student attention to the lab task does not match her sense of what is most appropriate for this lesson. As an expert teacher and expert thinker she first notices her own awareness, remembering how she might have responded in her first years of teaching. She quickly scans the class to gather additional information to formulate her next decision. She controls the impulse to admonish students for their behavior. The wisdom of experience has taught her that when students are off-task, there might be something wrong with the task itself. These thoughts and the monitoring of these thoughts all occur in split seconds as she mentally sorts out possible issues and possible actions.

Moving to the center of the lab, she calls for a pause in the action and calmly asks selected students to describe the source of their confusion. This action restores a sense of order and purposefulness to the room. By noticing and controlling her thinking, this master teacher is able to resolve this issue and smoothly extend student learning. Had she reacted impulsively, without monitoring and controlling her inner responses, she might have broken the lesson flow by contributing to student distraction and breaking momentum for all involved.

---

## An Expert Teacher's Professional Lenses

The knowledge base on teaching is both wide and deep (Saphier, Haley-Speca and Gower, 2008). For our purposes, we are organizing it here within five broad perspectives. We draw on the work of Lee Shulman (1987) for the first four: knowledge of the structure of the discipline(s); self; teaching skills and strategies; and learners and learning, and have added a fifth -- knowledge of collaborative work.

These five lenses offer frameworks for exploring growth areas for teachers. They provide organizers for the supervisor to structure learning-focused conversations with a teacher; to set learning goals; and to assemble resources for supporting and sustaining growth in personal and craft knowledge.

## Learning-focused Supervision: Developing Expertise

## Knowledge of the Structure of the Discipline

Teacher knowledge of the structure of a given content discipline correlates highly with student success in that area. This understanding moves beyond content knowledge alone and into the organization of knowledge within each domain. The structure of the discipline means knowing the big ideas within a content area; the organizing principles, key concepts and the ways in which they influence one another. In elementary mathematics, for example, understanding means being able to explain and illustrate a sense of number and how various operations such as addition and subtraction relate to each other. In social studies, it means showing students how to apply geographic, political, historical, economic and social perspectives to a given situation.

These deeper understandings greatly influence lesson design and lesson flexibility so that students can develop meaningful cognitive maps of their own (Darling-Hammond, 1997). When teachers have fragmented understandings themselves, they transfer these to their students and contribute to student misconceptions within that content area.

Teachers with rich structural knowledge are more flexible and resourceful in meeting the challenges that arise during classroom lessons. Real learning is messy. Students do not always fit neatly within the boundaries of lesson plans. Therefore, teacher content knowledge must always be greater and more complexly structured than that of their students. This allows teachers to prioritize and select those content objectives most appropriate for their students.

During planning and reflecting conversations, supervisors need to listen carefully for gaps in a teacher's understanding of important curricular ideas. Creating a climate in which it is safe for a teacher to ask for help with content understandings is a necessary condition for growth. No one knows everything about a discipline. This is especially true for elementary teachers and others who teach more than one content area. Providing resource materials and including mini-tutorials during conversations reduces anxiety and at the same time helps to ensure content accuracy for that teacher's students.

It is important for teachers to understand and be able to model the specialized ways of thinking in a given field. Literature and physical science, for example, each have their own principles of inquiry. In social studies, ideas are organized in specific ways. Mathematics has a rich problem solving repertoire. Writing narrative text is different than writing expository text. Each of these ways of knowing is a rich element within its content area.

By promoting these skills and perspectives, teachers help students discover how those who produce knowledge and knowing in a specific domain develop and modify ideas. So, too, do supervisors create these understandings for the teachers with whom they work.

Each content area is a minefield of misconceptions. Experienced teachers learn to anticipate these as they appear within curriculum topics. Their lesson plans reflect this thinking as they design ways to surface and dispel these barriers to deeper understanding. Knowing which misconceptions are developmentally appropriate at certain stages of learning is valuable craft knowledge. Knowing how to help students work through them is even more useful. The blend of content knowledge, learner knowledge and teaching knowledge that connects subject matter to targeted learning strategies is called pedagogical content knowledge (Shulman, 1987). Expert teachers assemble and draw upon a rich collection of analogies, models, memory aids and explanatory approaches to represent ideas and understandings to their students. They also develop tricks-of-the-trade for helping students to grapple willingly with misconceptions and to accept these as part of the learning process. One study of first year biology teachers noted that when the novices were presenting topics with which they had great depth of knowledge, they let their classes explore ideas as they asked questions that were more open-ended and promoted richer classroom discourse. When the novices were less confident of their own content knowledge, lessons were structured more rigidly the teachers themselves talked more and asked lower cognitive level questions (Carlson, 1991).

Helping teachers anticipate likely misconceptions and sharing instructional solutions is one way that supervisors increase effective practice. It is important to remember that individual teachers approach each subject differently (Shulman, 1987). For elementary teachers this means the ways they approach specific content areas such as reading or mathematics. For secondary teachers this usually means specific topics within a curriculum.

A teacher's approach to specific subject areas is a special consideration for supervisors of both elementary and secondary teachers. The choice of stance—coaching, collaborating, consulting or calibrating may need to be weighted differently for different content areas or curriculum topics. While teachers encounter a general set of universal challenges, content specific issues need to be analyzed for possible interventions. If classroom management issues crop up at specific times of day, the teacher's comfort with a specific subject area maybe an element to consider.

A supervisor's own content knowledge is a factor here as well. We all have our stretch areas. Sharing these with a teacher communicates a belief in lifelong learning. It is possible that the teacher may have content strengths to share with the supervisor and can contribute to mutual learning in that manner.

## Knowledge of Self

Knowledge of self includes the territories of conceptual, ego and moral development. It also includes knowledge of the personal values, beliefs and standards that guide daily decision-making. If teachers are to be effective with an increasingly diverse student population, they need to recognize and understand their own worldviews before they can appreciate and honor the worldviews of their students (McAllister & Irvine, 2000, Lindsey, Robins & Terrell, 2009).

Values and beliefs shape the perceptions and judgments that carry teachers through their days. They undergird the goals teachers set for themselves and for their students. Beliefs and values are the most influential element in the type of classroom culture and learning environment that teachers develop with their students (Pajares, 1992).

Beliefs about the nature of learning and the purposes and process of teaching shape curricular and instructional preferences. These beliefs also shape personal standards for what students should learn and the desired qualities of student performances and products. In what ways is learning about the transmission of important cultural knowledge and the development of basic skills? In what ways is it about developing students' thinking and problem solving skills and capacities? In what ways is it about developing a just society infused with democratic principles? In what ways is it about helping students discover and reach for their full potentials as human beings? And in what ways is it about promoting students' ethical and spiritual development (Eisner, 1994)?

These goals often overlap. In the heat of teaching and with the press of the clock and calendar, each teacher makes decisions about what to emphasize and what to let slide. These choices are at heart a matter of values and beliefs. Bringing these to conscious attention helps a teacher navigate conflicting options and the sometimes conflicting goals he or she encounters when his or her own beliefs bump headlong into institutional beliefs and values. Current stages of adult development influence how each teacher resolves these dilemmas. Caring supervisors support these explorations as vital lessons on the road to developing confidence and expertise as a teacher.

Knowledge of one's own learning style preferences is a special area of self-knowledge. It is important for teachers to realize that their preferred style may not be that of all of their students. Some of us perceive and process the world globally. Others prefer more sequential approaches. Some of us are task-driven and others are relationship driven. Some of us are visually dominant and others orient towards kinesthetic or auditory processing strategies (Guild & Garger, 1998).

All these style preferences, and the many subtle ways they manifest themselves, appear in our teaching. The ability to stretch against one's own preferred style is the hallmark of flexibility and the mark of a master teacher who can connect with a wide variety of learners.

Style is also an important area for supervisors to consider in their interactions with teachers. Flexibility in approach is especially important when the supervisor and the teacher have very different learning style preferences. The supervisor needs to remember that these are preferences and that the most resourceful people can stretch and flex as needed. It is also useful to remember that under stress we revert to our most dominant learning styles. This means that supervisors need to be especially aware of this dimension during times of predictable stress during the school year. It is also an important consideration when a teacher has had a particularly trying experience and needs to process it.

The reflecting conversation, offers an opportunity for sorting out the dilemmas and tensions teachers encounter in their daily work. Blocks or confusions in thinking are often a sign that a teacher has encountered a situation with students, parents or colleagues that violates some deeply held value or belief. This belief may not have consciously surfaced yet, but it is at the heart of this particular matter. A skilled supervisor will focus the conversation by exploring tensions from the teacher's point of view to help him

or her discover the values that he or she perceives are being violated. With self-knowledge as a frame, the supervisor and teacher can then pursue other perspectives and possible approaches to the situation. The supervisor may also need to take a consulting stance to share other viewpoints and alternative explanations that have not occurred to the supervisor.

## Knowledge of Teaching Skills and Strategies

Expert teachers, like concert violinists, consciously develop their performance repertoires. They assemble and hone microroutines that are combined and applied to fit a wide variety of conditions and settings. Master teachers automatize many routines and basic moves to free cognitive space for more sophisticated sensing of the needs of their learners. Such unconscious competence is the mark of an expert in the classroom. The lack of automaticity with basic moves, such as getting and maintaining student attention, giving clear directions and establishing routines for smooth classroom transitions, consumes the emotional and physical energy of many low-performing teachers. This is why these and other areas of basic classroom management are usually the first level of concerns addressed in the supervisory relationship. Until these fundamentals are under control, there is often little space for more sophisticated investigations of instructional practice.

Lack of comfort in these arenas blocks teachers' openness to ideas and resources that address other areas of teaching practice. It is often useful to front load face-to-face time at the beginning of the school year to share practical strategies and routines that work well.

Content specific pedagogy is an important variable that increases student success (Wenglinsky, 2000). Students whose teachers help them to develop higher-order thinking and problem solving skills linked to specific content areas outperform students whose teachers only convey lower-order skills (McLaughlin & Talbert, 1993). Supervisors support this essential part of the developmental journey and also extend the teacher's skills during planning conversations when they inquire into these elements. This is a place where the consulting stance adds great value at the point in the conversation when specific teaching techniques are being considered.

## Knowledge of Learners and Learning

Knowledge of who learners are and how each learns best guides the special relationship between teacher and students. The greatest teaching repertoire in the world is wasted if it is not well matched to the needs of learners (Saphier, Haley-Speca & Gower, 2008). The push for smaller class sizes and smaller schools is a response to the need to know one another. In an increasingly diverse world, personal knowledge and close relationships help to connect learners to teachers, to important ideas and to each other.

The exploding knowledge base about brain development, learning styles, multiple intelligence, developmental differences and cultural patterns energizes Lee Shulman's conception of the need for pedagogical learner knowledge on the part of all teachers (Shulman, 1987). Developmental differences extend far beyond the primary grades. Over the years, these differences amplify as the span between students widens in

Piagetian terms. There are many middle school and high school students who operate at a solid concrete operational level. These learners often run headlong into a curriculum organized by abstractions introduced through symbol systems. When teachers recognize these learning patterns and they approach instruction flexibly, they begin lessons and units with concrete experiences, then help students represent ideas with pictures and graphics as they support student language development and meaning making. This pathway leads students to firmer conceptual development and richer understandings of abstract ideas (Lipton & Wellman, 2000).

Given a changing student population, there is an increasing need for culturally respectful approaches to teaching and learning. Materials and methods that engage one population of learners may confuse or offend another. There is an important overlap here for teachers between this area and knowledge of self. How a teacher came to know an idea or discipline may not be an appropriate or effective cultural match for the students to which he or she is now teaching that same material.

Language differences are emerging as an important variable for teachers to consider. There is a critical variance between students' social discourse and their formal knowledge of the structure and norms of academic discourse in specific content fields (Lee & Fradd, 1998). Skilled teachers help students bridge their own language to formal academic language, integrating personal and cultural relevance with content understandings. This learning is more robust and more likely to be retained by students. This concept means that ultimately all teachers, no matter what their content specialties, are teachers of language and teachers of thinking.

## Knowledge of Collaboration

Knowledge of the why's and how's of collaboration is a hallmark of expert practice. Developing expertise in teaching is a joint venture. By participating in communities of practice, teachers expand and energize their own learning which in turn enhances the learning of their students. In powerful professional communities, the work of teaching and the craft knowledge for doing it skillfully are collective property. Studies of the best school systems in the world note well-developed patterns of high-quality, collaborative, professional engagement. In these settings, teachers work together to improve their own and others' instructional skills (Barber & Mourshed, 2009). Productive teacher teams regularly gather evidence of student learning and use these data to evaluate and modify instruction to target their students' learning needs (Hattie, 2009).

Successful collaboration requires and develops the knowledge, skills and dispositions for learning with and from colleagues. An essential value is that working with others is an important part of the work not something that keeps teachers from their work. In healthy collegial cultures professionals take collective responsibility for all of their students' learning and understand the links to how their own ways of working drive improvements in student performance. Ongoing cycles of assessment, inquiry and analysis, pattern-seeking and planning provide teachers with a fine-grained sense of the cumulative effects of shared practices (Lipton & Wellman, 2012).

Expert collaborators have practical knowledge of how adults work and learn together in groups. They know how to contribute to the learning of others and how to develop ideas and resource with their fellow professionals. Productive peer interaction takes

courage as teachers navigate the vulnerabilities and insecurities of opening their physical and metaphorical classroom doors to the scrutiny of others.

Structuring and supporting the growth of teachers as colleagues is a critical supervisory responsibility. This is an important arena for applying the Continuum of Interaction during learning-focused conversations with individuals and teams.

## Supervision as a Professional Vision

As supervisors gain experience and perspective on the craft of supervision, they gain new insights into themselves as teachers and as learners. This learning occurs on multiple levels. On one level, supervisors develop richer understandings about the craft of teaching. While engaging in personal reflection and articulating their own knowledge base to teachers, they deepen and integrate personal knowledge about professional practice. On another level, supervisors revisit their own history as teachers as they monitor the growth of teachers and come to see the parallel between this journey and the journey all learners take in any new field of endeavor. Yet on another level, the supervisor is learning about the art of supporting teachers. This, too, becomes a voyage of discovery in the passage from novice to expert supervision.

# References

Bandler, R. & Grinder, J. (1971). The structure of magic. Palo Alto, CA: Science and Behavior Books.

Barber, Michael, and Mona Mourshed. "Shaping the Future: How Good Education Systems Can Become Great in theDecade Ahead. Report on the International Education Roundtable." Singapore: McKinsey & Co., July 7, 2009. www.mckinsey.com/locations/southeastasia/knowledge/ Education_Roundtable.pdf.

Brandsford, J., Brown, A. and Cocking, R. (Eds.) (1999). How people learn: Brain, mind, experience and school. Washington DC: National Research Council.

Calderhead, J. (1996). Teachers: Beliefs and knowledge. In D. Berliner & R.C. Calfee (Eds.), *Handbook of Education Psychology* (pp 709-725). New York: Simon & Schuster MacMillan.

Carlson, W.S. (1993). Teacher knowledge and discourse control: Quantitative evidence from novice biology teachers' classrooms. *Journal of Research in Science Teaching*, 30 (5), 471-481.

Chang, F.Y. (1994). Schoolteachers' moral reasoning. In R. Houston (Ed.) *Handbook of research on teacher education* (pp 291-310). New York: Macmillan.

Chester, M.D, & Beaudin, B. Q. (1996). Efficacy beliefs in newly hired teachers in urban schools. *American Educational Research Journal*, 33 (1), 233-257.

Clark, C.M. & Peterson, P.L. (1986). Teacher thought processes. In M.C. Whittrock (Ed). Handbook of research on teaching (3rd ed) ) pp 255-296). New York: Macmillan.

Costa, A, & Garmston, B. (2002). Cognitive coaching: A foundation for renaissance schools. Norwood, MA: Christopher-Gordon.

Darling-Hammond, L. (1997). The right to learn. San Francisco: Jossey-Bass.

Danielson, C. (2011). The framework for teaching evaluation instrument. Princeton, N.J., The Danielson Group.

Ebmeir, H. (2003). How supervision influences teacher efficacy and commitment: An investigation of a path model. *Journal of Curriculum and Supervision*, Winter 2003. 18(2), 110-141.

Elgin, S. (2000). The gentle art of verbal self-defense. New York: Prentice-Hall.

Eisner, E.W. (1994). The educational imagination: On design and evaluation of school programs. New York: Macmillan.

Glickman, C.D. & Gordon, S.P. (1995). Supervision of instruction: A developmental approach. Boston: Allyn and Bacon.

Goddard, R., Hoy, W. & Hoy, A. (2000). Collective teacher efficacy: Its meaning, measure, and impact on student learning. *American Educational Research Journal*. Summer 37(2). 479-507.

Guild, P.B. & Garger, S. (1998). Marching to different drummers. Alexandria, VA: Association for Supervision and Evaluation.

Grinder, M. (1997). The science of nonverbal communication. Battleground, WA: Michael Grinder and Associates.

Hattie, J. (2009). Visible learning: A synthesis of over 800 meta-analyses relating to acheivement. New York: Routledge.

Hayakawa, S. I. (1964). Language in thought and action. NY: Hartcourt, Brace & World.

Holland, P, & Garman, N. (2001). Toward a resolution of the crisis of legitimacy in the field of supervision. *Journal of Curriculum and Supervision*, Winter 2001. 16(2), 95-111.

Hunt, D.E. (1976). Teachers' adaptation: Reading and flexing to students. *Journal of Teacher Education*, 27, 268-275.

Hunt, D.E. (1981). Teachers' adaptation: Reading and flexing to students. In B. Joyce, C. Brown, & L. Peck (Eds). *Flexibility in teaching*. New York: Longman: 59-71.

King, P. & Kitchener, K. (1994). *Developing reflective judgment: Understanding and promoting intellectual growth and critical thinking in adolescents and adults.* San Francisco: Jossey-Bass.

Lee, O., & Fradd, S.H. (1998). *Science for all, including students from non-English-language background. Educational Researcher,* 27 (4), 12-21.

Leithwood, K. Louis, K.S., Anderson, S, & Wahlstrom, K. (2004). How leadership influences student learning. New York: The Wallace Foundation.

Lindsey, R., Robins, K., Terrell, R. (2009). Cultural proficiency: A manual for school leaders, 2nd Ed., Thousand Oaks, CA, Corwin

Lipton, L. & Wellman, B. (2000) Pathways to understanding: Patterns and practices in the learning-focused classroom. Sherman, CT: MiraVia LLC.

Lipton, L. & Wellman, B. (2012). Got data? Now what?: Creating and leading cultures of inquiry. Bloomington, IN: Solution Tree.

McAllister, G. & Irvine, J.J. (2000). Cross-cultural competency and multicultural teacher education. *Review of Educational Research,* 70 (1), 3-24.

Marshall, K. (2009). Rethinking teacher supervision and evaluation. San Francisco, CA: Jossey-Bass.

Marzano, R. (2012). The Marzano teacher evaluation scales. Marzano Research Laboratory.

Marzano, R., Pickering D., & Pollack, E. (2001). Classroom instruction that works: Research-based strategies for increasing student achievement. Alexandria, VA: Association for Supervision and Curriculum Development.

McLaughlin, M. & Talbert, J. (1993). Contexts that matter for teaching and learning: Strategic opportunities for meeting the nation's education goals. Stanford, CA: Stanford University Center for Research on the Context of Secondary School Teaching.

Motluk, A. (2001). Read my mind. New Scientist, Vol. 169 issue 2275 :22.

Pajares, M. F. (1992). Teachers' beliefs and educational research: Cleaning up a messy construct. *Review of Educational Research,* 62 (3), 3007-332.

Rizzolatti, G. & Arib,M. (1998). Language within our grasp. *Trends in Neuroscience,* vol. 21:188.

Rowe, M.B. (1986 January-February). Wait-time: Slowing down may be a way of speeding up! *Journal of Teacher Education*: 43-49.

Saphier, J., Haley-Speca, MA., & Gower, R. (2008). The skillful teacher: Building your teaching skills. Acton, MA: Research for Better Teaching.

Sartain, L., Stoelinga, S., & Brown, E. (2011). *Rethinking teacher evaluation in Chicago: Lessons learned from classroom observations. principal-teacher, conferences, and district implementation.* Chicago: Consortium on Chicago School Research at The University of Chicago Urban Education Institute.

Shulman, L. (1987). Knowledge and teaching: Foundations of the new reform. *Harvard Educational Review,* 57 (1), 1-22.

Swanson H., & O'Connor, J., & Cooney, J. (1990). An information processing analysis of expert and novice teachers' problem solving. *American Educational Research Journal,* 27 (3), 533-556.

Schon, D.A. (1983). The reflective practitioner: How professionals think in action. New York: Basic Books

Schon, D.A. (1987). Educating the reflective practitioner San Francisco: Jossey-Bass.

Tschannen-Moran, M., Hoy, A. & Hoy, W. (1998). Teacher efficacy: Its meaning and measure. *Review of Educational Research.* 68(2) 202-248.

Wak, L. (2010). Two types of interpersonal listening. *Teachers College Record,* Volume 112 Number 11, 2010, pp 2743-2762.

Wenglinsky, H. (2000). How teaching matters: Bringing the classroom back into discussion of teacher quality. Princeton, NJ: Educational Testing Service.

References

# Learning-focused Supervision:
## Developing Professional Expertise in Standards-Driven Systems

# Exercises

# Mix, Match, Exchange

*Name* _____

- *One thing I find stimulating in my work:*

- *One thing I find challenging in my work:*

- *A belief I hold about learning-focused supervision:*

------------------------------------------------------------------------------------------------------------

*Name* _____

- *One thing I find stimulating in my work:*

- *One thing I find challenging in my work:*

- *A belief I hold about learning-focused supervision:*

## Think & Write

*As you consider developing learning-focused relationships,*
*what are some goals you are setting:*

• *For yourself?*

• *For your supervisory relationships?*

*What are some things to which you will pay attention to determine your success?*

# Nine Strategies for Learning-focused Consultation

*Examples*

## Offer a Menu

If one idea is useful, several are even more effective. Suggesting multiple options when planning or problem-solving (we suggest at least three) provides information and support while leaving the choice making, and the responsibility for making that choice, with your colleague. This might sound like: *"Given your concerns about developing meaningful homework assignments, here are three options to consider...."*

## √ Think Aloud

JJust as in instructional problem solving or modeling strategic reading strategies for students, sharing the thought process along with a solution or idea enhances the learning and maximizes the likelihood of transfer to future applications. This might sound like: *"When I encounter student confusions like this I first search for the underlying knowledge gaps and thinking patterns that might be contributing to those confusions. Then I try to figure out the instructional building blocks that will help develop essential understandings. So, in this case, you might look at ways to scaffold your students' understandings of these objectives."*

## √ Share What, Why and How

When sharing expertise, an effective verbal pattern is describing the 'what, why and how of an idea or suggestion. This might sound like: *"Here is a strategy for addressing that issue* (what)*; which is likely to be effective because* (why)*; and this is how you might apply it* (how).

## ┼ Refer to Research

Referring to specific research-based best practices is often a productive consultation strategy. This approach offers expert advice drawn from credible sources that can be applied to the current situation. This might sound like: *"The research on having students create graphic representations has been very consistent across grade levels and content areas. One application of those ideas to consider here would be to teach your students how to develop cause and effect diagrams to illustrate the important relationships in this history lesson."*

## State A Principle of Practice

Connecting a specific strategy or solution to the broader principles of effective practice provides an opportunity to learn and apply the principle, as well as the individual idea, in other situations. This might sound like: *"An important principle of practice related to (topic) is _____; so a strategy like (suggestion) should be effective in this situation."*

## √ Generate Categories

Ideas or solutions as categories provide a wider range of choice and a richer opportunity for learning than discrete strategies or applications. For example, a category such as 'grouping students' is broader than 'putting students in pairs' or suggesting a specific partnering strategy. This approach is especially effective when categories are offered as a menu. This might sound like: *"Several broad categories of successful classroom management include attention moves, establishing routines, maintaining momentum and developing effective transitions between activities."*

## Name Causal Factors

Rather than suggesting potential solutions, it can be very productive to offer several factors that might be producing the problem. This option is particularly effective when working with experienced teachers. This might sound like: *"There are several things that typically would produce that behavior (or result); for example _____, _____ or _____."* Followed by a shift to a coaching stance to add: *"Given what you know about your situation, what's your hunch about which of these, if any, might be an influence?"*

## $+$ Consider an Alternative Point of View

Effective problem solving can be stimulated by an exploration of multiple perspectives. When idea generation bogs down, surfacing additional points of view can re-energize the conversation. For example offering thoughts on how parents might consider the issue, or administrators, or the students, and so on. This might sound like: *"It is possible that your students are not perceiving the purposes of the new reward system in the ways that you had intended. It might be effective to consider their beliefs about motivational rewards."*

## ✓Reframe the Problem or Issue

Expert problem solvers spend a greater amount of time defining a problem than they do strategizing solutions. Novel approaches to the problem definition not only release new energy and ideas, but often lead to a more effective solution. Related to considering alternative perspectives, reframing is changing the context or representation of a problem; including positive or useful aspects of the issue and alternative descriptions of the goal or approach to the problem. This might sound like: *"There are several ways to think about classroom climate and culture. Typically teachers search for simple rules and fair consequnces to apply equally.  Another approach might be to work from the inside out and support students in developing the self-management skills to be productive classroom citizens and contributing group members."*

*Examples*

# Paraphrasing: Increasing Confidence and Consistency

## Acknowledge and Clarify
*Emotions and Content*

- So, you're feeling _____
- You're noticing that _____
- In other words _____
- Hmmm, you're suggesting that _____

1. This concept is really tough to teach at this grade level. It requires a degree of intellectual development that I don't think all kids have at this age.

2. I'm not sure that all parents are ready to support the new homework policy. It's a real break with tradition that is sure to upset those people that want our policies to still be like things were when they were in school.

3. I have a kid in my 3rd period class that is really getting to me. I think he stays up at night thinking of ways to provoke me. He knows he gets to me and that upsets me even more.

4. Today's lesson really went well. It was the first time that the cooperative groups really worked well together both socially and academically. I hope we have more days like today.

## Summarize and Organize

*Stating themes and big ideas, separating confusing or jumbled ideas.*

- So there seem to be two key ideas here _____
- On the one hand _____ and on the other _____
- For you then, several themes are emerging _____
- It seems you're considering a sequence or hierarchy here _____

1. What a day I've had! The kids were all wound up by the change in the schedule --- I hope that settles down soon. And on top of that, the network went down today and I had to scramble to run my lesson without Internet access. It's really frustrating when you take time to plan for technology integration and there are so many student and technical variables.

2. Jerome's mother is coming in to see me tomorrow and I'm really worried. He's basically a good kid, but he's slacking off and not paying attention in class. I need to figure out what's going on for him but I'm not sure his mother and I are seeing things the same way.

3. I finally figured out how to teach that lab on density in a way that helps kids get the concept and not get lost in all the math and measurements. But, wow does it take time to do it right. Now, I'm behind in the curriculum with kids who are finally more confident as science learners.

4. Developing good formative assessments sure takes time both in their creation and then in the scoring. I think it's ultimately going to be worth it in terms of student learning but there is sure a lot of upfront work for teachers and teams.

## Shifting Level of Abstraction --Up

*Reframing the speaker's language to a higher level of abstraction*

So, a(n) _____for you might be _____
- category or concept
- value
- belief
- assumption
- goal
- intention

1. I really love teaching expository writing. It's really about helping students learn to think clearly and express those thoughts in interesting ways. When kids care about the topic and have something to say, it's rewarding to help them find their voice and communicate ideas effectively.

2. We just had the worst meeting of the year. People were all over the place --- no one stayed on the topic and people kept interrupting one another. If our students behaved that way we'd stop things and talk about respect and effective process. I'm at a loss as to why our classroom norms don't transfer to the meeting room.

3. This new social studies unit still needs work. The materials are disorganized and the major concepts are not stated clearly. I practically have to revise each lesson from scratch to sort it out for the next day. This really should have been field-tested better before it was dropped on us.

4. I don't know why my students aren't doing better with reading comprehension. I've been working on building background knowledge and teaching them strategic reading skills and they still are struggling when I check for understanding or give them short quizzes.

## Shifting Level of Abstraction --Down

*Reframing the speaker's language to a lower level of abstraction*

So, a(n) _____for you might be _____
- example
- nonexample
- strategy
- choice
- action
- option

1. I really love teaching expository writing. It's really about helping students learn to think clearly and express those thoughts in interesting ways. When kids care about the topic and have something to say, it's rewarding to help them find their voice and communicate ideas effectively.

2. We just had the worst meeting of the year. People were all over the place --- no one stayed on the topic and people kept interrupting one another. If our students behaved that way we'd stop things and talk about respect and effective process. I'm at a loss as to why our classroom norms don't transfer to the meeting room.

3. This new social studies unit still needs work. The materials are disorganized and the major concepts are not stated clearly. I practically have to revise each lesson from scratch to sort it out for the next day. This really should have been field-tested better before it was dropped on us.

4. I don't know why my students aren't doing better with reading comprehension. I've been working on building background knowledge and teaching them strategic reading skills and they still are struggling when I check for understanding or give them short quizzes.

# Crafting Goal Paraphrases

*Construct a paraphrase to respond to each of the following statements. Check your language for its invitational quality. Be particularly aware of positive presuppositions.*

1. I don't understand why these kids aren't more engaged in their work. I design interesting lessons, I'm enthusiastic and I work hard. Its all very demoralizing!

2. My principal visits my classroom every day and I'm worried about what she's thinking. I don't know where I stand with her or if she even likes me.

3. This curriculum is confusing for my students. The concepts are too abstract and inappropriate for this grade level and the activities don't make sense.

4. Parents only contact me when they have a complaint or concern. It seems like no one notices all the good things going on in my classes and all of the positive things that I'm doing for their children.

# Paraphrasing: Shifting the Level of Abstraction

With your partner, craft a shift level of abstraction paraphrase (up or down) for each example.

1. I think that I need to spend more time working on the deeper conceptual building blocks of math with my primary students to build a firmer foundation of understanding and less time on computational practice. I hope that I can get parents to understand why this matters.

2. My students really got excited when we held a debate about global warming. They really dug in and did their research on the environmental data, the economic implications and the political issues.

3. My grade level team is struggling when we work with student performance data. We tend to hold back any comments that might appear to be criticism of each other. We all know that this is going on but we can't seem to move through it.

4. I have a student this year who is making me crazy. He's really bright but he's only doing just enough work to get by. In fact, he seems to be calculating the exact grades he needs to get on each assignment to maintain a passing score. I think he's really enjoying the game.

# INVITATIONAL INQUIRY

| INVITATION | COGNITION | TOPIC |
|---|---|---|
| How might . . . | Predict | Outcomes |
| What would . . . | Recall | Curriculum |
| What are some . . . | Summarize | Instructional strategies |
| What might be some... | Identify | Student readiness |
| In what ways . . . | Describe | Student behavior |
| How might you . . . | Compare | Student work |
| What seem(s) . . . | Contrast | Student engagement |
| Given your . . . | Prioritize | Performance standards |
| Based on . . . | Interpret | Assessment results |
| Reflecting on . . . | Infer | Expectations |
| As you . . . | Conclude | Lesson |
| | Generalize | Materials |
| | Connect | Groups |
| | Apply | Classroom climate |
| | Evaluate | Procedures |

## EXAMPLES

What are some ways you are comparing this student's work to the performance standards?
(Invitation) (Cognition) (Topic) (Topic)

Recalling your concerns, how might you address this student's behavior?
(Cognition) (Invitation) (Topic)

As you consider these assessment results, what seem to be priorities for next steps?
(Invitation) (Topic) (Invitation) (Cognition)

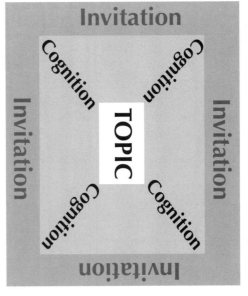

### The Elements of the Invitation:

• Attending Fully
• Approachable Voice
• Plural Forms
• Exploratory Language
• Nondichotomous Forms
• Positive Presuppositions

Sample Stems

Given your knowledge of...
Based on your experience with...
Reflecting on...
As you consider...

Syntactical Substitutions

• the------some
• could----might
• is------seems
• why-----what

## Try This

### Embedding Positive Presuppositions When Asking Questions

Identify the presupposition(s) in each of the following questions. Consider the intention of the question, and rewrite a question that communicates positive presupposition.

| | |
|---|---|
| 1. Do you have any hands-on materials for this lesson? *EXAMPLE: Given that manipulatives are effective learning tools for introducing math concepts, what are some hands-on materials that might work for this lesson?* | 5. Why did you choose that goal? |
| 2. Can you think of any reasons for that behavior? | 6. When do your students usually get the objective? |
| 3. What two things would you change about this assignment? | 7. Have you tried graphic organizers for these lessons? |
| 4. At what point did you notice the lesson wasn't working? | 8. Did you see the students in the back that were texting? |

# Developing Teacher Expertise • Inquiry Exercise

## Managing Classroom Procedures

Elements include:
• Management of instructional groups • Management of transitions • Management of materials and supplies

| From Present Practice | To Desired Practice | Inquiry |
|---|---|---|
| Some instructional time is lost due to only partially effective classroom routines and procedures. | There is little loss of instructional time due to effective classroom routines and procedures. | |
| The teacher's management of instructional groups, transitions, and for the handling of materials and supplies is inconsistent, leading to some disruption of learning. | The teacher's management of instructional groups and/or the handling of materials and supplies is consistently successful. | |
| With regular guidance and prompting, students follow established routines. | With minimal guidance and prompting, students follow established classroom routines. | |

## Communicating with Students

Elements include:
- Expectations for learning
- Directions and procedures
- Explanations of content
- Use of oral and written language

| From Present Practice | To Desired Practice | Inquiry |
|---|---|---|
| The teacher's attempt to explain the instructional purpose has only limited success, and/or directions and procedures must be clarified after the initial student confusion. | The instructional purpose of the lesson is clearly communicated to students, including where it is situation within broader learning; directions and procedures are explained clearly. | |
| The teacher's explanation of the content may contain minor errors; some portions are clear while other portions are difficult to follow. | The teacher's explanation of content is well scaffolded, clear, and accurate and connects with student knowledge and experience. | |
| The teacher's explanation consists of a monologue, with no invitation to the students for intellectual engagement. | During the explanation of content, the teacher invites student intellectual engagement. | |
| The teacher's spoken language is correct; however, vocabulary is limited or not fully appropriate to students' ages or backgrounds. | The teacher's spoken or written language is clear and correct. Vocabulary is appropriate to students' ages and interests. | |

## Engaging Students in Learning

Elements include:

- Activities and assignments  • Grouping of students  • Instructional materials and resources  • Structure and pacing

| From Present Practice | To Desired Practice | Inquiry |
|---|---|---|
| Learning tasks and activities are partially aligned with the instructional outcomes but require only minimal thinking by students to be passive or merely compliant. | Learning tasks and activities are aligned with the instructional outcomes and are designed to challenge student thinking, resulting in active intellectual engagement by most students with important and challenging content and with teacher scaffolding to support that engagement. | |
| The lesson has a recognizable structure; however, the pacing of the lesson may not provide most students the time needed to be intellectually engaged. | The lesson has a clearly defined structure and the pacing of the lesson is appropriate, providing most students the time needed to be intellectually engaged. | |
| | | |

## Using Questions, Prompts and Discussion Techniques

Elements include:
- Quality of questions/ prompts
- Discussion techniques
- Student participation

| From Present Practice | To Desired Practice | Inquiry |
|---|---|---|
| The teacher's questions lead students along a single path of inquiry, with answers seemingly determined in advance. | While the teacher may use some low-level questions, he or she poses questions to students designed to promote thinking and understanding. | |
| The teacher attempts to frame some questions designed to promote student thinking and understanding, but only a few students are involved. | The teacher creates genuine discussion among students providing adequate time for students to respond and stepping aside when appropriate. | |
| The teacher attempts to engage all students in the discussion and to encourage them to respond to one another, with uneven results. | The teacher successfully engages most students in the discussion, employing a range of strategies to ensure that most students are heard. | |

## Try This

Review the following examples. Identify the vague language. How might you inquire for more specificity?

In what ways would this tool be useful to a learning-focused supervisor?

1. These kids never do their homework!

2. Parents don't care.

3. My students are always wild.

4. I'm not ready.

5. I have to do this.

6. This strategy is better.

# Questions that Focus Thinking • Inquiry Exercise

**Managing Classroom Procedures**

Elements include:
- Management of instructional groups • Management of transitions • Management of materials and supplies

| Teacher | Paraphrase | Inquiry |
|---|---|---|
| My kids do great working in groups. I love to give them team tasks and watch them go to it! | | |
| I can't seem to get my students to focus. We waste so much time just taking attendance and settling in each morning. | | |
| My class usually responds very quickly to signals. But some students just aren't with the program yet. | | |

## Engaging Students in Learning

Elements include:
- Activities and assignments   • Grouping of students   • Instructional materials and resources   • Structure and pacing

| Teacher | Paraphrase | Inquiry |
|---|---|---|
| I spend hours making games and learning activities for my kids and they still don't participate in the lesson. Just yesterday, I was teaching patterns so I brought in checkers. | | |
| None of my students are really motivated to read in social studies. When they finish their reading, I ask questions but I don't get very many hands up. Maybe I should do some kind of reward? | | |

## Using Questions, Prompts and Discussion Techniques

Elements include:
- Quality of questions/ prompts
- Discussion techniques
- Student participation

| Teacher | Paraphrase | Inquiry |
|---|---|---|
| When I ask a question, the same students raise their hands. How can I get more kids to participate? | | |
| I don't like group work. When I put my students into groups, one or two end up doing all the work. | | |
| This is a great strategy. My students really like it. | | |

# Inquiry Exercise

| | Data | Inquiry |
|---|---|---|
| 1 | Several students are texting under their desks while Mr. T is explaining the problem on the whiteboard. After several minutes he notices these behaviors and says "Would it help if I text the problem to you?" Two of the students put their smart phones away; two do not. | Based on your experience with this class, how typical is this student response pattern? -------------------------------------------------------------------------- -------------------------------------------------- Given your experience with classroom management, what might be some alternative choices for correcting inattentive behavior? |
| 2 | The objective is clearly written on the board in Ms. M's 5th grade classroom. She begins the lesson with a ten-minute lecture on the land rush using a timeline and a US map for visual reference, with no mention of the learning objectives. | What were some indicators that your students were clear about the objective and the expectations for learning in this lesson? -------------------------------------------------------------------------- -------------------------------------------------- As you were describing the land rush, what were some indications of students' understanding of the content and connections to the posted objective? |
| 3 | "This is hard, but most of you will be able to do it." Teacher circulates among students as they are working. Student 1.: "Mr. P, I can't figure this out." Mr. P "Just do the best you can." Student 2: "Mr. P, I'm not sure if I've got this." Mr. P "You've solved these kinds of equations before, think about the variable here." | |
| 4 | Ms. J claps three times; 15 of 24 students clap back. She directs students to their small groups. Five of the groups move to tables and choose a materials manager within 4 minutes, ready for next directions. When Ms. J is ready to describe the task, one group (of six) is not yet in place. | |
| 5 | As students are entering the room, Ms. G smiles, greets them and directs them to the problem on the board. Some students get right to work, others go to their seat but don't take out materials, still others are milling in the back of the room sharing stories about their weekend. Without addressing the standing students, Ms. G moves to the board and begins the lesson. | |
| 6 | Ms. H has projected a snapshot of student writing on the whiteboard for a demonstration lesson on editing. However, the image clarity and print size is impossible for the students to read. She keeps the students in place at their desks rather than inviting them to move forward. | |

| 7 | The objective is clearly written on the board in Ms. M's 5th grade classroom. She begins the lesson with a ten-minute lecture on the land rush using a timeline and a US map for visual reference, with no mention of the learning objectives. | |
|---|---|---|
| 8 | Mr. J asks his first grade class:<br>"Who can give me an example of a mammal?" 20 or 22 hands go up. One student is called on and says "dog".<br>"Who can give me an example of a reptile?" Same 20 students volunteer. A different student is called on and says, "snake".<br>Finally, Mr. J asks, "What are some differences between mammals and reptiles?" Four hands go up. | |
| 9 | Dr. W demonstrated a chemical reaction. Lab partners are completing a short answer worksheet. Some examples include: "What materials were used?" "What was the evidence of reaction?" "What conclusions are you drawing?" | |
| 10 | Mr. N is moving about the classroom while students write responses to the prompt on the board based on a reading assignment. He is occasionally praising ('good job, nice work'), occasionally correcting ('this needs a capital', 'this is an incomplete sentence') and occasionally suggesting ('you need a transition word', use more vivid language') as he circulates. | |
| 11 | Ms. Z's second graders are reading about a text on weather. She asks for a thumbs-up signal to the question "What is one type of weather?" 17 of the 21 students show a thumbs-up, but her sampling reveals only 2 correct examples. She directs them all to re-read the text more carefully. | |

## Try This

### From Description to Thoughtfulness

Each of the questions below are requests for information. Rewrite the inquiries to increase thoughtfulness.

| | |
|---|---|
| 1. How many students will you put in each group?<br>EXAMPLE: *What are some criteria you use to determine group size?* | 5. How will you build technology into this lesson? |
| 2. Which text will you use for this lesson? | 6. How many of your students complete their homework? |
| 3. What strategies will you use to capture students' attention? | 7. How many minutes do you spend on full group instruction? |
| 4. How will you reward students for excellent effort? | 8. How often do you change your classroom displays ? |

# Try This

Teacher: My challenge is trying to figure out how to keep, how to support the students that need it and enrich the students that have the knowledge, and be able to keep them growing so that they stay engaged and challenged throughout the school year.

Directions: Craft a paraphrase of each type in response to the presenting statement of the beginning teacher you viewed in the Video Clip.

Acknowledge and Clarify

Summarize and Organize

Shift Level of Abstraction

## The Continuum of Learning-focused Interaction

| Supervisor/Specialist | Information, analysis, goals | Information, analysis, goals | Teacher |
| --- | --- | --- | --- |
| | CALIBRATING          CONSULTING | COLLABORATING          COACHING | |

| Know | Think I know | Want to know |
| --- | --- | --- |
| | | |

| Scenario | Stance Shifting |
|---|---|
| In this middle school math lesson, the teacher's objective is: Students will analyze properties of plane geometric figures in order to identify properties of angles, parallel, and intersecting line segments. Students will view a local neighborhood map and identify parallel, intersecting and right angled streets, using their own geometric solid shapes, rulers, colored pencils, paper, math book as reference.<br><br>Please show me the right angles, how about the ones that are not right angles?<br><br>Where will you put your solid figures?<br><br>Can you show me an acute angle? | Coaching Inquiry |
| How about your parallel streets?  Perpendicular?<br><br>I can't wait for you to show your work…<br><br>You are doing such a good job! | Consulting Strategy |
| We are coming up on 15 minutes, and I love what I see---I'm going to choose a couple that are making progress, and are about 75% done… take about 5 minutes<br><br>(As T moves among pairs, students show her their work, and she asks them to point out the features, parallel, intersecting, right angles, etc.) Let's give this pair a big hand for their work… | Coaching Inquiry |

| Scenario | Stance Shifting |
|---|---|
| In a sixth grade lesson, the teacher's stated objective is, "Students will understand tone and mood, and the tools an author uses to get the reader to feel something and get to know the characters."<br><br>How many have seen the movie Mary Poppins? (8 hands up) What do you think the tone was that the author intended? (1 hand up: tired of kids being spoiled) ok, turn and talk at tables, what is the mood of Mary Poppins? (Table talk for 35 seconds) 5,4,3,2,1<br><br>What kind of feeling, emotion, attitude were they trying to give you? ------waiting------ | Coaching Inquiry |
| (One st) ok, Christian (stuff's not always perfect) T writes on board<br><br>Ok so quickly, you will watch the preview. What is the author trying to convey in the preview---what is the feeling they are trying to get you to feel?<br><br>T displays the preview of M Poppins<br><br>What kind of emotion did they convey? (1: happiness)<br><br>What else? Caitlin (sadness) what part was sad?<br><br>What else? (cheerful) what made it cheerful, Josh? | Consulting Strategy |
| Aria? (dancing and singing) that made it cheerful… | Coaching Inquiry |

# 3-2-1          + 1

| | |
|---|---|
| 3 | |
| 2 | |
| 1 | |

# Exploring Student Work Products

Directions: Ask teachers to collect samples of student work (in a given content, over a specified period of time works well). Ask processing questions such as those below to stimulate thinking.

MATERIAL COLLECTED (Work Sample(s):

## Cognition: Identification

What are some things you're noticing about _____?

What are some examples of _____you see in this work?

## Cognition: Cause-Effect

What's your hunch about student readiness/ preparation and the quality of this work?

What are some choices you made that led to the success of this product?

## Cognition: Analysis

How does this student's work compare to what you might have predicted?

What are some patterns you're discovering across these student work samples?

How do these work samples compare to standards (internal and external)?

# Reflections, Connections, Directions

| Topic | Reflections<br>What I remember | Connections<br>For me/my work | Directions<br>Action/steps I will take |
|---|---|---|---|
|  |  |  |  |

# Learning-focused Conversations: Reflecting Journal

## Activating and Engaging

### Recollections
As you reflect on this event (e.g., lesson, workshop, meeting) what are some things that come to mind?

### Perspectives and Perceptions
In this event, what was particularly satisfying?

In this event, what were some things that concerned you?

*Based on your experiences today, what might you:*

• Stop doing

• Continue doing

• Start doing

**Name:**                                              **Date:**

## Learning-focused Supervision Skills: Primary Trait Rubric

**Purpose:**  This self-assessment organizes specific attributes and skills for applying the Continuum of Learning-focused Interaction and for each element in the linguistic toolkit.  It is intended to provide baseline data for feedback and personal goal setting.

**Directions:**
1. Record a learning-focused conversation and create a transcript.  Complete the rubric without the aid of any print material.
2. For each rating, please cite specific "evidence" from your transcript.

**Unaware:** I don't know what this means.
**With Prompts – or When I remember:** Need visual support material on hand
**Fluent:** Consistent use  - regular application of the stance/tool in multiple circumstances
**Flexible:** Full integration - can access full repertoire of tools responsively/ can differentiate use based on context

## Self-Assessment:  Navigating the Continuum of Interaction

| Continuum of Interaction | Unaware | With Prompts or When I Remember | Fluently | Flexibly |
|---|---|---|---|---|
| I can define, describe the purpose of and distinctions between each stance<br>-   Coaching | | | | |
| -   Collaborating | | | | |
| -   Consulting | | | | |
| -   Calibrating | | | | |
| I can apply strategies for each stance:<br>-   Coaching | | | | |
| -   Collaborating | | | | |
| -   Consulting | | | | |
| -   Calibrating | | | | |
| I understand when and why I would navigate to another stance | | | | |
| My verbal and non-verbal language is congruent with my stance | | | | |

## Self-Assessment: Attending Fully

| **Attending Fully**<br>Be fully present and: | **Unaware** | **With Prompts or When I Remember** | **Fluently** | **Flexibly** |
|---|---|---|---|---|
| Listen without interruption | | | | |
| Listen without<br>- Personal Listening | | | | |
| - Detail Listening | | | | |
| - Certainty Listening | | | | |
| Listen for assumptions, inferences, problem frames, perceptions, perspectives | | | | |

## Self-Assessment: Inviting Thinking

| **Inviting Thinking**<br>Use Invitational Elements which include: | **Unaware** | **With Prompts or When I Remember** | **Fluently** | **Flexibly** |
|---|---|---|---|---|
| An approachable voice (intonation) | | | | |
| Plural Forms | | | | |
| Exploratory Language | | | | |
| Non-dichotomous stems (eliminate yes/no) | | | | |
| Positive presuppositions | | | | |

## Self-Assessment:  Sustaining Thinking

| **Pause**<br>Pause to allow time for thought | Unaware | With Prompts or When I Remember | Fluently | Flexibly |
|---|---|---|---|---|
| - After asking a question | | | | |
| - After teacher's initial response to allow time for additional information | | | | |
| - Before paraphrase | | | | |
| - After paraphrase to consider strategic next move | | | | |

| **Paraphrase**<br>Apply paraphrases preceded and followed by a pause, that: | Unaware | With Prompts or When I Remember | Fluently | Flexibly |
|---|---|---|---|---|
| - Acknowledge & Clarify content and emotion | | | | |
| - Summarize/Organize comments | | | | |
| - Shift Level of Abstraction up | | | | |
| - Shift Level of Abstraction down | | | | |

| **Inquire**<br>Construct inquiries that: | Unaware | With Prompts or When I Remember | Fluently | Flexibly |
|---|---|---|---|---|
| Include Elements of the Invitation | | | | |
| Use language to focus on specific cognitive processes | | | | |
| Use data to inform questions | | | | |
| Explore cause-effect | | | | |

| | | | | |
|---|---|---|---|---|
| Ask questions that produce new insights and applications | | | | |
| Ask questions to surface specific examples | | | | |
| Ask questions to clarify explanations, ideas, deletions, generalizations | | | | |
| Ask questions to examine inferences, assumptions, implications, consequences | | | | |

**Learning-goals:**

Based on my assessment,

| My Goal | Achievement Indicators | Strategies/Action Steps | Completion by |
|---|---|---|---|
| | | | |

# Learning Partners

Make an appointment with 4 different people—one for each icon. Be sure you each record the appointment on your page. Only make the appointment if there is an open slot at that spot on each of your forms.

_____

_____            _____

_____

# Notes

# Notes

1-7-16

promente sentence stems

# Notes

# Notes

# About the Developers

Laura Lipton, Ed.D is co-director of MiraVia, LLC, a multifaceted training and development firm dedicated to creating and sustaining learning-focused educational environments. Laura is an international consultant whose writing, research and seminars focus on effective and innovative instructional practices and on building professional and organizational capacities for enhanced learning. Her educational experience includes K-12 classroom teaching in both special and general education. She has been a district-wide reading resource coordinator and staff development director for a consortium of 37 school districts in the New York metropolitan area.

Laura's publications with Bruce Wellman include Groups at Work: Strategies and Structures for Professional Learning, Data-driven Dialogue: A Facilitator's Guide to Collaborative Inquiry, Mentoring Matters: A Practical Guide to Learning-focused Relationships and Pathways to Understanding: Patterns and Practices for the Learning-Focused Classroom. Additional publications and articles include More than 50 Ways to Learner-centered Literacy (with Deb Hubble); Supporting the Learning Organization: A Model for Congruent System-wide Renewal (with Ruth Greenblatt); Shifting Rules, Shifting Roles: Transforming the Work Environment to Support Learning (with Arthur Costa and Bruce Wellman) and Organizational Learning: The Essential Journey (with Robert Melamede).

Laura can be contacted at:
236 Lucy's Lane • Charlotte, VT • 05445
P. 802-425-6483 • F. 802-329-2341 • e-mail: lelipton@miravia.com

Bruce Wellman is co-director of MiraVia, LLC. He consults with school systems, professional groups and agencies throughout the United States and Canada, presenting workshops and courses for teachers and administrators on learning-focused classrooms, learning-focused supervision, presentation skills and facilitating collaborative groups. Mr. Wellman has served as a classroom teacher, curriculum coordinator and staff developer in the Oberlin, Ohio and Concord, Massachusetts public schools. He holds a B.A. degree from Antioch College and an M.Ed. from Lesley College.

He is author and co-author of numerous publications related to organizational and professional development, learning-focused schools and classrooms and group development. His publications include: Groups at Work: Strategies and Structures for Professional Learning (with Laura Lipton), Data-driven Dialogue: A Facilitator's Guide to Collaborative Inquiry (with Laura Lipton); The Adaptive School: A Sourcebook for Developing Collaborative Groups (with Robert Garmston); Shifting Rules, Shifting Roles: Transforming the Work Environment to Support Learning (with Arthur Costa and Laura Lipton); and Mentoring Matters: A Practical Guide to Learning-focused Relationships and Pathways to Understanding: Patterns & Practices in the Learning-Focused Classroom, (both with Laura Lipton).

Bruce can be contacted at:
229 Colyer Rd. • Guilford, VT • 05301
P. 802-257-4892 • F. 802- 257-2403 • e-mail: bwellman@miravia.com

# Professional Development Programs and Services

## Putting Theory into Practice in Your Schools

MiraVia provides learning-focused
professional development programs and services
that present practical strategies, useful resources and innovative ideas
for thoughtful educators grappling with critical professional issues.

## Seminars • Keynotes • Consulting Services

### Developing Learning-Focused Relationships

**Target Audience:** Teacher mentors, instructional and content coaches, curriculum specialists and instructional supervisors

**Explore** the essential concepts, templates and mediational tools for developing effective, learning-focused relationships between growth-oriented educators.

Workshops and seminars include:

- Mentoring Matters: A Practical Guide to Learning-Focused Relationships
- Learning-Focused Relationships: Coaching, Collaborating and Consulting for Professional Excellence
- Learning-focused Supervision: Developing Professional Expertise in Standards-Driven Systems

### Building Professional Community

**Target Audience:** School and district leaders, site and district teams, facilitators and group developers

**Learn** critical skills for developing collaborative school cultures that focus on the learning needs of students and the adults who serve them.

Workshops and seminars include:

- Got Data? Now What?
- Data-Driven Dialogue: Facilitating Collaborative Inquiry
- Leading Groups: Framing, Presenting, Collaborating and Facilitating
- Learning-Focused Presentations
- The Facilitator's Toolkit: Balancing Task, Process and Relationship
- Teacher to Teacher: Working Collaboratively for Student Success

### Creating Learning-Focused Classrooms and Schools

**Target Audience:** Beginning and experienced classroom teachers, staff developers, instructional leaders

**Discover** the bridge between current learning theory and effective classroom practice. Our research-based and classroom-tested Pathways Learning Model offers a coherent framework for organizing lessons and units of study.

Workshops and seminars include:

- Pathways to Understanding: Patterns and Practices in the Learning-Focused Classroom
- Pathways to Literacy: Reading and Writing in the Content Areas
- Getting Started, Getting Smarter: Practical Tools for Beginning Teachers
- Thinking to Learn, Learning to Think

 Based on our book of the same title

## About  The Road To Learning

*mira (L.)[MIR-â]: wonderful/amazing   via (L.)[VE-â]: way or road*

I N 1596, the German astronomer Fabricus saw a third magnitude star in the constellation Cetus, the Whale. As they continued to observe it over the next century, astronomers became aware of its unusual fluctuations, now brighter, now fading, and honored it with the name Mira, the Wonderful.

As a partnership dedicated to continued development for professionals, we connect the constancy of presence and fluctuating brightness with the learning process. We believe that learning means working through the temporary dullness of not knowing, while pursuing the brilliance of new understanding. Our name, and our philosophy, combines this wonder of learning, Mira, with Via, or the road. Our publications, products and seminars offer pathways to professional insight and growth.